PRAISE FOR FINDING HER VOICE & CREATING A LEGACY

"I hugely enjoyed reading a book that's seriously additive to the literature in our field."

– Jay Hughes
author, researcher, and current active Fellow of Wise Counsel Research Foundation

"The hallmark of wealth, it is said, is complexity. This research shines a spotlight on the unique complexity experienced by women who are family leaders and wealth holders. This book joins the growing chorus of research that says wealth is far from toxic—it can be empowering. You will be inspired."

– James Grubman PhD
author and internationally-recognized consultant to families of wealth,
family enterprises, and the advisors who serve them

"This groundbreaking work has enabled us to hear from these fascinating women— in their own words—as to how they found their way, and their voice, within the complicated dynamics of successful families."

– Kristi Kuechler
former President of the Institute for Private Investors and
Managing Director, Family Office Exchange

"This research is groundbreaking. The power is in the stories shared, and lessons derived to support women of wealth that came directly from their contemporaries."

– Mariann Mihailidis
Principal M2 Connections and Research Fellow at Wise Council Research

"Amy is a great storyteller whose enthusiasm is infectious, and I thoroughly enjoyed her presentation. You are a great storyteller, and the stories you told were wonderful."

– Joel Pineles
SFO

"These powerful stories are a gift to share with our next generation leaders. They provide insights about the importance of women in leadership and how they strengthened the roots of their family and business over time."

– Caroline Coleman Bailey
Founder & Chief Emotional Officer of Premier Growth

"These stories of grit, love, determination, vision, patience, and persistence are so needed. They are the story keepers and peacemakers and their contributions within the family system represent a welding link between the generations. I hope this book becomes the catalyst for deeper study and programming."

– Dave Specht
Director, Drucker School Global Family Business Institute

"This book serves as both a celebration of the women who have united and empowered their families and family enterprises and as a road map for men and women alike who hope to be the integrators, developers, and innovators that drive harmony and success across a business or down through generations."

– Jim Coutre
Vice President, Insights and Connections

"So many times, the women in family businesses are overlooked and their essential contributions under-valued. This book brings these women and their stories into the spotlight. I hope that readers will see that the myth of the heroic solo entrepreneur is truly that—a myth. No family business of any generation survives and thrives without the support and leadership of spouses, mothers, and daughters."

– Marion McCollom Hampton
Senior Partner, Banyon Global

PORTRAITS OF PIONEERING WOMEN
LEADING WEALTHY FAMILIES

FINDING
her voice
& CREATING
a legacy

BY AMY HART CLYNE
AND DENNIS T. JAFFE

A Pitcairn Publication

Finding Her Voice & Creating a Legacy
Portraits of Pioneering Women Leading Wealthy Families
Amy Hart Clyne and Dennis T. Jaffe
Copyright ©2021 by Amy Hart Clyne and Dennis T. Jaffe

Published by Pitcairn
165 Township Line Road, Suite 3000
Jenkintown, PA 19046
www.pitcairn.com
www.findinghervoice.com

Identifiers:
ISBN 978-0-578-92535-6 (paperback)
Library of Congress Control Number: 2021913139

Cover and book design by Craig Rogers

ACKNOWLEDGEMENTS

Many people contributed to this project. It represents many voices. First, all the women who were interviewed contributed their wisdom, their candor, and their deep concern for the development of the emerging roles for women family enterprise leaders.

Many people helped us locate women to participate and commented on early drafts. They include: Stacy Allred, Helen Antoniou, Debbie Bing, Hugh Braithwaite, Ella Chase, Jim Coutre, Kim Eddleston, Jim Ethier, Jane Flanagan, Jim Grubman, Marion Hampton, Madeline Levine, Kathryn McCarthy, Jackie Merrill, Michele Mikeska, Natasha Pearl, Nicola Roigard, Kirby Rosplock, David Specht, Christian Stewart, and Susan Winer.

A special thank you to Leslie Voth, Chair and Chief Executive Officer of Pitcairn for her support of this essential work. Leslie has dedicated her career to serving these women and their families, truly listening, and partnering with them to support their personal and family growth. She is an exemplary female trailblazer who is inspiring a new generation of leaders.

DEDICATION

I dedicate this book to my own mother, Patricia. She was a pioneer in her own right, and I can trace my lifelong passion for learning and family back to her unending warmth, strength, and love. To my incredible family, Tim, Kathryn, Megan, and Peter, I extend my love and gratitude for their endless support. To all the new matriarchs and amazing women in my life, especially my extraordinary sister Eileen and my best friend Tracy. Thank you for inspiring me every day and being there for me in moments both large and small.

Finally, I dedicate this book to our readers, especially the young women still seeking their paths. May this work spark passion, inspire action, and give you confidence and clarity in the journey to find your own voice.

– Amy

I dedicate this to my family, my wife Cynthia, my sons and their incredible life partners, and my grandchildren. We are a family where women have always been teachers and leaders, and they have given so much to me and the other guys.

– Dennis

contents

FOREWORD:
WHO ARE TODAY'S WOMEN
OF WEALTH?

It's a question that's increasingly asked, but difficult to answer without defaulting to a persona wrapped in an enigma. These women control a large percentage of the world's wealth; oversee a significant portion of today's philanthropic programs and perspectives; and play an increasing role in shaping the philosophies and priorities of future generations.

Yet, what do we really know about them? We may know their names, but we rarely hear about their experiences and perspectives directly.

Far too often, their stories are told through the lens of others: their husbands, their children, outsiders, or even the media. The rare times they're included, it's often in bland recountings of family business origin or by third or fourth generation family members who never knew them as real people.

Our research for this study was specifically designed to address this narrative oversight, which has left one of the most important family voices in some of the world's most influential families sidelined or silenced. For generations, they've remained elegant, effective, and ever elusive. But their stories must be told. Their voices must be heard. The positions they hold in the enduring sagas and generational successes of wealthy families are every bit as essential as their patriarchal counterparts—maybe even more so.

Our methodology was both anthropological and cultural—revolving around conversations, not data points. We've spoken in depth with many women of considerable means about how they came to wealth, their role in the family, the obstacles they overcame, and how they prepared their rising generation while sustaining family connections and family harmony.

No surveys, no panel discussions, no publicity filter. Just intimate, in-depth conversations in which women could share their stories honestly and anonymously. A chance to reflect on what's shaped their lives and the role they've played in influencing the lives of others.

Breaking new ground on such an important topic has been tremendously rewarding. It's been one of the great pleasures of my career to talk to these women and hear and share their stories. It's our hope that this research begins to form a foundation of new thinking and a new focus on women of wealth. Even more, we hope it catalogs and catalyzes a movement.

Since our first undertaking, we've expanded our ambitions for this project to now include conversations with more women from more walks of life around the globe.

At the same time, we'll continue to mine our existing conversations for further insights and share those findings and their implications for various stakeholders.

But the real power of this research comes from the stories themselves. We've been afforded a unique and exclusive opportunity—the chance to hear women who have achieved tremendous success share how they found their voice and created their legacy. These women are role pioneers for the modern-day, painting their portraits through challenging, complex, often circuitous journeys.

Please join in reframing a more human and accurate narrative about women of wealth that celebrates and honors their enduring contributions to their families—and our world.

Amy Hart Clyne
Pitcairn Chief Knowledge & Learning Officer

INTRODUCTION: WOMEN'S EVOLVING ROLE IN FAMILIES OF WEALTH

Women's roles are changing.

Across the globe, women are accelerating their ascension to positions of power and influence as well as amassing significant wealth.

As of March 2021, 41 women are leading Fortune 500 companies, from fashion-forward beauty and clothing conglomerates to organizations in the typically male-dominated industries of motor vehicles and financial services. These standard bearers are illustrative of women's growing role in shaping history through power and influence.

At the same time, women control more wealth than ever before. In 2019, there were eleven self-made female billionaires worldwide.[1] Just one year later, there were one hundred. Across countless corners of society, women have passed a tipping point to where staid stereotypes and traditional roles are fading fast.

But, in the exclusive enclave of ultra-high net worth families, the roles of women remain hindered by longstanding conventions and complex intergenerational dynamics. The mythical heroic patriarch looms large in many wealthy family histories, often relegating women to supporting roles and rarely giving them a voice in their own story. These traditions, combined with lingering societal inequalities, have created a complicated path forward for women of wealth today.

Yet, these women share in the accomplishments and ambitions that have defined the gender dynamics of the 21st century. As women gain more power and prominence in their own families and throughout society, these women of wealth remain a critically underserved group, their stories and experiences sorely lacking from the broader picture of female empowerment and accomplishment.

We set out to uncover the voices and perspectives of this elusive group at this critical time. For our research, we took an anthropological approach that gave us the opportunity to hear these women's stories in their own words.

What we uncovered were stories universal yet unique; eloquent in their recitation and extraordinary in their outcomes. Individuals experiencing the triumphs and tribulations shared by so many women while at the same time navigating massive fortunes and complex legacies. Women who found ways to make marriages work, families flourish, and businesses thrive.

These stories serve as the foundation for powerful findings that offer a fresh and meaningful new look at women's roles in families of significant wealth. It brings them out of the shadows and shines a spotlight on their convictions and their contributions.

It shows them not as subservient wives and daughters, but complementary and assertive partners and parents. These findings have powerful implications for affluent families as well as the industries that serve them.

We're grateful to the women who have taken part to date for their time, insights, and courage in sharing their journeys. Our research reveals that these women often define success by a different set of metrics than their husbands and use a different set of skills to realize it. They're partners and peacekeepers. Caregivers and co-investors. Agitators and arbitrators. Visionaries and voices of reason.

Women, from their own perspective, have made significant gains over the past century on their way to finding success and fulfillment. Women's right to vote was the infant moment of subsequent change, and they slowly discovered greater business opportunities and became more accepted in financial, business, and political positions. And in marriage, they began to be treated as less subordinate to their husbands.

Women's progress has accelerated greatly over the past fifty years. With the passage of the Equal Credit Opportunity Act in 1974, women no longer needed their husband's permission to get credit. Regarding family finances, sisters began to inherit equally with their brothers. Also, modern medicine permitted women greater reproductive rights and more control over childbearing. As for education, opportunities broadened as colleges accepted more women, so that by 2017 women comprised 57 percent of undergraduate students.[2] But today, even though women comprise more than half of the student body at both medical and law schools, they occupy only a small percentage of top executive and financial positions. Nonetheless, women's lives and the opportunities available to them have progressed significantly over the past hundred years, which has meaningfully changed the calculus of how women consider their own roles vis-à-vis their families and their careers. Yet their journey is far from complete.

While gender differences are not destiny, women in families do perceive and act differently than men and tend to approach their work and lives in contrasting ways—even if this isn't clearly defined. Above all, women of wealth want to be treated fairly in relation to access and control of family wealth and have artificial barriers within the family removed. As this happens, women's power and influence within families will increase, although their approach to acquiring these benefits will differ from that of their male counterparts.

For this study, we interviewed thirty-four women in North America, half of them from the initial generation of family wealth and the rest from later generations. We interviewed each one for about ninety minutes. We asked them how they came to wealth, how their role in the family developed, what obstacles they overcame, and how they prepared their rising generation, all the while sustaining family connections and family harmony. For most of them, their minimum net worth was more than $500 million.

Since our research into the evolving role of women family leaders in families with significant wealth is happening during an era when the traditional role of "wife" and how she will be engaged with work and business is in deep flux, we acknowledge that we're seeing a snapshot of that role amid change. By comparing what we learned with traditional roles, we see that these women are role pioneers. They're setting aside traditional behavior and expectations and forging their own path. The transformation of a woman's role within a family of wealth can be especially challenging. By taking on huge responsibilities within their families and family enterprises, these female pioneers can become role models and teachers to other women. For this publication, women who are living through this evolution shared their experiences with us as they took on new roles and discovered their own power and influence.

Several studies document the emerging power and influence of women in relation to their financial success, whether through professional accomplishment, marriage, or inheritance. Yet, for all the successes that women have experienced, a recent global survey by Barclays[3] of four hundred wealthy families found that evolution to full equality still has a way to go. While women today are likely to inherit substantial wealth, the survey found that fewer than half of them were as involved in family investment, business, and other financial decisions as their male counterparts. But that's changing fast. The survey also found that while older generations held a patriarchal view of wealth—a belief that men should lead and make major decisions about business and family wealth—only a third of their children held such views.

A 2020 study by professional services firm KPMG[4] found that "while women continue to face the dilemma [of] role conflict, they're equipping themselves to balance the obligations at work and at home." It also found that even as women continue to take major responsibilities for their own families and the upbringing of their children, they're increasingly active in their family enterprises. For example, women in families of wealth are increasingly being considered for and offered leadership roles in various areas of their wealth structure. In another study[5], author Kirby Rosplock compared how men and women related to their family wealth.[6] While she found many similarities, she also discovered that women felt less knowledgeable, confident, involved, or in control of their wealth and decisions about it. Wives in enterprising families felt that they weren't full partners nor fully working together. The barriers to this weren't only internal but also originated in family and societal expectations.

While the arc of the evolution toward women's heightened role in the family is clear, being in the middle of change isn't always easy or pleasant. Many older family members hold more restrictive views of women's roles. And as women move into formerly male territory, claiming new authority, they face resistance from those who don't really accept that women can handle increased responsibility (although lip service is paid in this regard)—and from those who will lose power and influence in a shifting power dynamic.

As women's external roles change and evolve, there's a corresponding change in the development of their identity, how they see themselves and their options. It can be intimidating to take on a new role and risk entrance into the unknown. Being a pioneer isn't for the faint of heart, and the women we interviewed for this study had to tap their inner resources to move into new roles. Our interviews explored how they've brought meaningful change to their own family roles and created positive transformation within their families.

While women have always been the cornerstone of the household, they're increasingly moving into leadership roles within family operations. But as you'll see, that path is circuitous, complex, and often controversial—although it takes place largely in the privacy of business and financial families. Our goal is to open a window into this largely hidden process, and to offer a picture of how it takes place and how it affects the women, their families, and their emerging, rising generations.

Our work illuminates the evolving role of women as leaders and influencers in the realm of family enterprise—the term we use to refer to all the assets in a family such as an operating company(ies), investment portfolios, philanthropic initiatives, or a family office. It's a project that began with our seeing that women, whose roles in family wealth matters were murky up to a point, were becoming more and more active in making critical family decisions, not just about family but also about their wealth. Their voices emerged with such power and influence—and were received with such respect and admiration in their family ecosphere—that we became delighted by and very curious about their journeys.

Women with whom we crossed paths were often caught in a struggle for authority in their family enterprises. They felt pressure to fulfill traditional expectations as mothers while at the same time becoming increasingly concerned and interested in how the presence of wealth and a family enterprise influenced the wellbeing of their family and children. They wondered if other women felt the same tension and what those women, whether they be older or younger, were doing about it. We also heard inspiring, creative efforts in some families to manage these crosscurrents.

We were overcome by the generous and honest sharing of these women, who were motivated by their willingness and ability to share with us what they were learning. While their families were private and their challenges were personal, they were deeply committed to helping us help other women, partly because few, if any, of our women contributors had many or any formal role models in their journeys.

Our work also illuminates the varied ways in which families experience wealth. Some families sell their legacy business and invest the resulting profits in other ventures and assets—ranging from family vacation homes and real estate to extensive portfolios of investments. Many also "invest" in philanthropic and social ventures, while others have the support of their own family office. A family needs different kinds of leadership to maintain these diverse assets and sustain the family's identity in relation to various businesses, assets, and advisors. This diversity leads us to use the term "family enterprise" to refer to all shared family assets, not just a single family business.

> **Our work illuminates the vast differences framing families' experience with wealth. From liquidity events and real assets to social ventures and philanthropic causes, family enterprises encapsulate the diversity of family assets.**

Our approach can be labeled "appreciative" in that we were looking for positive stories that embodied creative solutions. We weren't trying to get a representative sample that we could generalize from, and we didn't seek out the disaster stories of family conflict and dissolution that are all too common. Instead, we wanted to uncover the exemplary stories of women who became excellent family leaders. Most of the women we interviewed were those with whom we've worked, or who were referred by colleagues; others, about one third, came from clients of Pitcairn, the sponsor of this research.

Initially, we called these women leaders "matriarchs"—a term that is defined as "a woman who is head of her family and a guide and role model for her descendants." It denotes an older woman who's venerated for her wisdom and strength as the leader of a family, attaining an almost mythic status in that family. The label has its roots in historical texts, but we found that some of the women we interviewed, especially those who were younger, rejected the label, as for them it evoked a dated concept of women as solely caregivers, mothers, or supportive spouses who exercise hidden, indirect influence. They felt that their roles were more individualized, complex, and far-reaching than the term implies. While we appreciate those views, we still have chosen to use this label as it is not meant to be pejorative but rather a badge of honor that we use in the most positive sense of the word. It applies most clearly to the older women who are part of the first generation of family wealth, though some women in later generations who have been family leaders for a while also fit the description. We see them as "new matriarchs", a role that will be defined as we share what we learned. We use the term to refer to the way that they've defined their role as spanning not just enterprise but also family stewardship, and to denote how this role is more extensive than the traditional role of male or female family business leader.

While they may be matriarchs in a traditional sense, these women, especially those in later generations, prefer to describe themselves simply as family leaders or "stewards"—doing what's needed to pass the family's accumulated wealth and achievements to a new generation. Their roles are often informal, sometimes not visible or public, and at times not noticed or heralded. They identify with the concept of stewardship, or servant leadership, referring to a type of leadership that listens closely to the needs of others and finds ways to move forward quietly, but inclusively. This is often in contrast to a view of leadership that's patriarchal and dominating. As you'll see, their roles are not confined to either business or family; their responsibilities span the business and the family, and their conception of family leadership often was defined as encompassing both.

Soon after we began the interviews, we saw that the women naturally fell into two groups: those new to wealth and inheritors of wealth. The newcomers were wives of business founders they had either worked beside to create the family enterprise or married later. The inheritors were in the second or later generations of family enterprises who were called upon to become successors and take on various roles of family leadership.

The first-generation, new-to-wealth women were all somewhat older: they were post-World War II children with an average age in their mid-seventies, and many were grandparents. The inheritors were more mixed in age, with an average in their early sixties, but all were over forty and parents themselves. Their role expectations, mindsets, and values were all shaped by the social dynamics of the late twentieth century, when women's roles were changing but progress tended to be in fits and starts. Their family members had both traditional and progressive views of the woman's role. None of the interviewees were from the millennial generation, and just a few represented Gen X—

whose perspective we expect to be very different since they will be more accustomed to equal roles and be the beneficiaries of the pioneering work and leadership of our study participants. Their stories should be the subject of future research.

With such a small sample, we cannot draw conclusions or generalize about "most" women family leaders. But the stories we heard from these visionary women offer a window into what's possible and can inspire others with their success. They shine a light on the internal challenges that arise when a woman moves into a leadership role and the creative ways in which they can exercise that role in traditional, male-focused families and cultures. They showed us not just what they do but also why they were called to act, how they reached their goals, and how it changed them and their family.

This publication contains two main sections, each centered around one of the generational groups: those new to wealth and the inheritors of wealth. Since their family and social realities were different as wealth acquirers or inheritors, we report their experiences separately, although there are also clear continuities in their approach to their roles and styles of leadership.[7] The first section highlights the hidden role of "the matriarch" in their first generation of wealth ownership. These women were new to wealth and faced the task of defining how the new wealth would be used and how new leadership would develop. The second reveals rising-generation women as family-culture innovators. In some ways, they continue the task started in the first generation, but they face the additional complexity of siblings and expectations different from the first-generation pioneers. We viewed their contexts and relationships to family business and wealth as different enough to merit treating them separately.

Together, these sections offer a picture of evolving family wealth and how women are taking on increasingly influential roles. We chronicle their unique paths and the impact they can make. Their influence is felt not only in the management of family wealth but also in how generations to come are being raised differently and offered greater and more equal opportunities.

We present their stories as a gift to women from wealthy families who face their own futures with difficult choices that affect not just their own lives but also those of their husbands, siblings, and children. Their stories also help and inform the advisors who interact with them. The enormous interest in this body of work has led us to believe that we've started an extraordinarily important conversation, even a movement—one that will widen and drive women's opportunities in business and family in every successive generation. We hope to attune women of wealth and their advisors to a continually changing and improving process of social evolution. What exists today will be very different a generation from now. We can dimly imagine, but remain hopeful for, an end point when gender-neutrality and full equality in access to leadership roles and role flexibility is achieved.

Our hope is that there will be greater recognition of how women have contributed so significantly in the families of the extraordinarily wealthy, and the key role they've played in creating extraordinary families. Further, our hope is that these stories will inform and inspire the next generation of women leaders in families of wealth and that the hard lessons learned in the past will prove instructive and supportive.

These are their stories, told in their voices, based on their life and family experiences.

PART I

new to wealth

1

FIRST-GENERATION WOMEN STARTING LIFE JOURNEYS

The predominant origin myth of a family business is that of a heroic entrepreneur almost single-handedly creating a company through the force of his skill, vision, and presence, overcoming obstacles at every turn. This isn't incorrect, but its heroic focus represents only one slice of reality. Alongside the wealth creator, often working in the shadows, is the spouse and life partner helping him and adding to his capability. The spouse contributes in many ways—as helper, sounding board, mediator, and primary parent in preparing the next generation—besides taking responsibility for the household and raising the children.

Part One of this publication defines the position they developed, their perspectives, contributions, and business roles. These women are first-generation owners, either because they married into wealth or partnered to create it. While sometimes their voices were unwelcomed or not actively solicited, they found unique, creative, and courageous ways to contribute as family leaders. Several of the women emerged as visible leaders after the death of their husbands.

Drawing from the experiences of fifteen North American ultra-high-net-worth women from the first generation of their family wealth, this first section of our study brings to life their multiple roles and tasks, and the nature of their relationships with their husbands, families, work, and advisors. Their stories can inspire other families about how women new to wealth contribute to the overall success and prospects of the family enterprise.

All but three of these fifteen women came into wealth as partners in founding entrepreneurial businesses; the others married into existing wealthy families. While their husbands were usually the public face of the wealth and the business, in many ways they were partners and collaborators in the effort.

Their average age is well into their 70s, so they're reporting on a long tenure, extending into their third generation. Eight of the women outlived their husbands and became business leaders after their passing. Four others were second wives, or married after wealth was created, but they played a role in how the family lived with its wealth and helped develop the next generation as responsible stewards. Some had prior professional careers and used their skills to advance the family enterprise. Their roles and future have been influenced by the times, during which the definition and opportunities open to women have been expanding.

This section follows the development of these women's roles as pioneers in wealthy families along several stages of their evolution. These include their experience in growing up and starting their life journeys; how the wealth-creating couple evolve their roles in developing the business; how the wife/mother prepares the rising generation to become family stewards or next generation leaders; how to overcome the unexpected loss of a partner and emerge as a widowed family leader; and, after remarriage and raising a stepfamily, how a blended family not only offers a challenging situation for a second spouse but also an opportunity for innovation. Let's begin with starting life journeys...

First-generation matriarchs evolved into role-altering pioneers through a lengthy process of societal influence and self-discovery, shaped by milestones of business success and off-ramps to prepare the rising generation for leadership and stewardship.

We found just a few differentiating themes from the early lives and upbringing of these women pioneers. Two-thirds came from poor or working-class families; the remainder came from professional or entrepreneurial families, which offered them some advantages. As for the families, some were loving and supportive, while others had abusive tendencies. Several of the women had a professional education— but we found nothing that presaged their future success.

However, these future matriarchs had two qualities in common: they all grew up with a fierce determination to work hard and take care of themselves. Those from poorer backgrounds, in particular, knew that they had to make it on their own. Rather than feel resentful or overwhelmed by their disadvantages, they reasoned that if they got a good education and worked hard, they could do better than their parents and achieve success. Also, they developed faith in themselves early—from being successful in high school to seeing part-time work as a path toward income stability. Some were the first woman in their family, or even the first person, to go to college.

Our subjects stressed that either through hardship or following the values taught by their parents (usually their fathers), they developed a strong work ethic. In other words, they were ready to make their own way in life. They all mentioned an intense inner drive, especially if they came from families of limited means. Some of the wealthier families of origin had more traditional expectations of their daughters. When one from a modestly wealthy family was told that women don't need to go to college, she responded by financing her schooling. Another was told not to get her own apartment after college, but she did it anyway.

Besides preparing to make their own way in life, they looked for life partners who shared their values. The strong sense of themselves and their worth translated to not seeing marriage and family as a rescue or a road to success. They always expected to work and contribute to family projects. While they looked for solid partners, it didn't appear they were looking for partners who would give them a life of leisure. They found spouses whose drive and work ethic they admired, reflecting their own values. They often had strong fathers, and they tended to look for spouses who would be strong, ambitious, confident, and self-defined, but not at their expense.

Looking at the early days of their marriages and businesses, the women seem quite traditional on the surface—perhaps because they mainly originated in working-class communities in the final decades of the last century. Most of them married fairly young. Indeed, four of them married childhood sweethearts. But after their marital partnerships started out with traditional expectations, they later diverged—because they were attracted to the vision, work ethic, and entrepreneurial energy of their husbands.

These results might seem at odds with the women's intentions to be independent and pursue their own paths, but each couple saw the business as a shared venture. The wife bought into the vision and instinctively knew that her drive and skill would play an important role in achieving success. Their division of labor sometimes emerged naturally, especially if the husband was charismatic or more outgoing. In that case, he could be the visionary, external salesman, and dealmaker, while she could build infrastructure and implement effective operations by tending to the culture and community of their employees. And so, instead of a company failing to deliver on a wonderful vision, these unconventional partnerships were able to develop every aspect of a business.

While traditional couples have complementary relationships with separate gender roles, more couples today have a marriage in which both partners work. But when children arrive, the wife usually takes responsibility for raising them. The couples we interviewed at first appeared to follow this path, but they quickly merged into more of a partnership. And as their confidence grew, these women each developed their own personal "brand" of leadership within the family, without which the family wouldn't last for generations.

2

INFORMAL BUSINESS PARTNERSHIPS AND COMPLEMENTARY ROLES

While the vision and drive of the entrepreneur are essential in creating long-term success for a family business, many other areas also kick in. The vision must be executed; a capable, dedicated and loyal staff must be recruited and sustained; a culture of goodwill and high performance has to be established; the family's children must be raised and developed into adults, preparing them to be part of the business or responsible owners; crises have to be mediated in the business and family alike; and a culture of shared values, cooperation, and excellent work must be sustained in business and family, both in good times and hard times.

Can one person accomplish all of this? Maybe. But accounts from key family participants show us that if we look behind the scenes, many actors help create success, even if most of the attention is focused on the wealth creator. Perhaps the most central of these actors is the wife or partner living and working alongside the founder. This person is able to see the links between founder, business, and family, offering skills and attention to those areas the founder may overlook.

To fully understand the success of a family business, we need to consider the couple that sits at its heart. In fact, given the small number of family businesses that survive long term, we can hypothesize that the presence of a capable partner who shares the vision and the work, and attends to some of the less-glamorous or less-visible areas, may be the "secret sauce" that ensures success. In a family, and in a business, there are official roles and other, non-public, informal ones. A wife may sit way in the background, without a formal role or any authority, yet, as we'll see, she can be an essential partner in the family enterprise.

Recognition—or even mention—of the nature and dynamics of this informal role is almost nonexistent. The late Léon Danco, perhaps the first person to call himself an advisor to family businesses, recognized the wife's role when counseling many founders. And in a book written by his wife, Katy, she made it clear that women are not just passive beneficiaries but also active advisors.[8] Also, a report by Ernesto Poza and Tracey Messer[9] (based on interviews, like this publication) emphasizes the complementary role of the spouse as a family steward, business advisor, and mediator across generations.

Many of their insights are affirmed by our work almost a generation later.

In regard to these complex relationships—in which a person can have one role in one social system (the family) with a certain level of authority while at the same time having a different, perhaps less powerful role in another (the business)— differences arise because of the differing nature of the roles and the fact that couples often have different concerns and capabilities[10]. There's also a related role in couples who act as formal co-leaders of the business—often defined as "copreneurs"—that's similar to the stewardship role we define here, with the addition of the venture's public recognition as a shared effort[11].

Partnership isn't necessarily recognized explicitly; in fact, it rarely is. One woman we interviewed, referring not only to her own role but also that of her husband's parents in a company where his father was CEO, observed, "It doesn't have to be a specific corporate role or title. The role of being a partner is so much more than just that."

The couples we spoke with pursue a vision, either the husband's or a shared one. They love the work, and love doing it together, but their drive to succeed isn't always to make money or get rich. Here are examples of the origins of a few couples' businesses: starting a winery with her husband, a winemaker who went out on his own after an investor, out of respect for his skill, was willing to become a silent partner; a husband worked in a car dealership until he convinced an investor to sell him a franchise with his wife's support despite their modest means; and a young couple who met at work started a financial services firm together.

Among these couples, the husband was typically designated the CEO, but actual business development was shared. The husband may have had the initial drive, but to succeed, the wife found there were many things that needed to be done that he had not considered. "Both of us came from backgrounds where money was not the focus of life, but we knew it was important," one woman said. "[So] we had to plan ahead, save for the future." This shared passion and support, as well as complementary skills and personalities, added to her husband's success.

While not intended or clearly recognized, the support role can be the differentiating factor in allowing a family enterprise to succeed. It often begins gradually out of need. For example, one wife found herself learning about the finances that her husband needed help with; and even with limited education, she was a quick learner. She organized his financials, and as the business grew, so did her capability. Listening to hers and the stories of other women, and knowing that many entrepreneurs fail, it's hard to imagine that success can even happen if male entrepreneurs do not have a capable and dedicated partner.

While not intended or clearly recognized, playing the supporting role wasn't one devoid of importance. In fact, in many ways it's the differentiating factor in allowing a family enterprise to succeed.

In some businesses we examined, the wife became an equal partner. In the winery, for example, the husband was a talented winemaker, but his business and financial skills were limited, so his wife filled in the gaps. She notes that there are three essential components of a successful winery—making the wine, marketing, and selling—while building the brand with good management and organization. Her husband was a master of the winemaking, but while they could have hired folks for the other areas, she found that she had the talent and energy to manage them herself.

In all three of the above cases—and indeed with all of the women who were business partners and subsequently widowed or divorced—they were unafraid of conflict because of the strong partnerships with their spouses. We observed that many of the female partner leaders, when called to make tough decisions, were willing to risk relationships and experience family rifts, likely something they learned from their spouse or perhaps their fathers. As their spouse, or daughter, they could challenge the leader from a base of love, trust, and respect, in a way that nobody else could. Their forceful conviction was notable and impressive because it was often unexpected traditionally.

The women we interviewed adopted one of three roles in relation to their husbands:

(1) a complementary one, pursuing a shared passion and vision, in which she often took on a specific role in the business, adding her skills to enhance the pair's capabilities;

(2) working behind the scenes on key tasks to achieve success, in which her impactful role was largely hidden; and

(3) pursuing her own independent career, while helping the business in visible but limited tasks out of concern for the family and the growing business.

Each role adds value to the business, sometimes in ways that are hard to measure, but becomes an important contributor to the overall success. The differences have to do with the visibility of the role and the degree to which the couple differentiate themselves. We present three stories here, each representing one of the above roles.

These roles extend the meaning of leadership power. These women have immense power and influence, but they exercise it without formal roles or authority, or informally behind the scenes. They aren't dominators but rather exercising what is called "soft power", or sometimes servant leadership. They lead by engaging others, starting with their husbands, and then others in the business and advisors. Their stories offer clear and vivid examples of how this form of power is so central to family enterprise.

STORY 1:
Complementary Roles

This woman created a special relationship with her husband to build a large and successful business while raising their five children and preparing all of them for an eventual future in the business.

Alice and Ben, who were each raised on farms, met while young. "Ben always wanted to have his own business," Alice said. "That was a goal that we talked about very early in our marriage, and we tried to save money to reach that goal." It was a goal to which Alice linked herself, and when a business came up for sale, she agreed they would move with their three sons to a new community for Ben to realize his dream. While working together in the business, they had two more sons. The whole family now works for the huge and successful business.

Alice went all out to help the family succeed. "That was one of my hardest challenges because I wanted to be a stay-at-home mom," she said. But she realized that the business needed help. "My husband is not a detail person, so I started out doing the accounts payable and then it just worked into where I was the accounting department for a few years until we had to get more help." She went back and forth between being home with her boys and working in the business, even setting up a crib in the office. She eventually became the HR person, interviewing and selecting employees.

While her role became more and more important to the growth and success of the business, she had an ambivalent view of herself in a leadership role. "I don't know if I saw myself as a leader, but I tried to improve my skills in that regard [she had not gone to college]," she said. "I loved all our people, all our team members. ...I enjoyed the work and enjoyed working with others and collaborating. But I, myself, was never really comfortable with being the leader. I like to be in the background and not be out in front of people much. ...I felt it was my job to make things work." Alice believed the key ingredients of making things work were collaboration, communication, and cooperation.

While Alice worked as a mother and a strategic partner in the business, Ben was perceived as the leader, though the staff turned to her for internal operational challenges. On raising her five sons, she was surprised when the first one, then all five entered the business. They seemed to have complementary skills and were comfortable working together. "I feel that we started a legacy," she said. At one point, she had to make a difficult decision with her husband and the other executives to select which of her sons should be the new CEO; and then she had to deal with her motherly feelings after the eldest wasn't selected. As a result, her family diplomacy skills, already important, were put to the test to enable a successful transition and keep her first son on board.

STORY 2:
Essential Confidante

This wife made a behind-the-scenes contribution, illustrating how wealth creators share responsibility and work as a team, even as the outside world sees the husband as the leader and creative force.

While growing up very poor with an abusive, alcoholic father, Pam had to take care of her family and earn money. Her grandmother helped support her and the family, and her mother was always pushing, but was cowed by her husband. The skills she learned by taking care of herself and her siblings enabled Pam to succeed in her adult role as a helpmate and parent. She hated high school and graduated early, at fifteen, and soon met her future husband, who was twelve years older. "He saved me," she said. He began his career running a store he inherited from his family, working hard with long hours. She became his everyday helper.

Working with an investor, her husband opened new stores and got twenty-five percent ownership if he opened a store on time, on budget, and with trained staff. Soon he had a minority ownership in a score of stores. "It was his dream, his vision. I was just along for the ride," she said. "And I just loved being with him and doing things with him. ...A lot of that was because he allowed me not only to be his confidante, not only his wife but [also] his brain in a lot of ways, because he would leave me with a task list every day. I'd get it done. If I ran into any snag, he'd help me through it." They were full partners from day one. She trained the staff and took care of the money. "He and I had such trust in each other that we knew that if one could think it, the other could do it," Pam added.

Her life as a parent began unexpectedly. One day she got very sick, which was unusual for her, and she was surprised to discover she was pregnant. So, Pam had to combine motherhood with supporting the business. "I'd take the children to the [office] building with me," she said. "I'd set up a playpen. Paula would play in it and Charlie would sit in his bassinet." Pam recounted a story about her kids playing together making "pretend soup." They saw some matches on their dad's desk and wanted to make the soup real— and unintentionally set a fire. The business was saved, but the story lives on.

Pam also talked about how she took steps to find ways to connect their busy father with the kids. While he wasn't always able to attend their sports events, she was able to get him to get off the grid on family trips by acquiring a large motorhome. These trips were special for all of them. Sadly, he died suddenly when their kids were teenagers. Amid her deep sorrow, Pam took over and grew the business. It was difficult for her. She struggled with depression; but with therapy and her dedication to the family, she continued to develop the business—and eventually created places for both her son and daughter to enter and continue the business.

STORY 3:
An As-Needed Partner

While pursuing her own career, and out of a desire to be helpful and meet a need, this wife's role evolved and eventually led to a greater and more formal role in the business.

During a successful professional career, Carlene began helping members of her husband's family who were running the business. When the business started to struggle, they called upon her to help with project after project, until she decided to leave her career and help build the business. "Eventually, I became like the COO," she said. "My husband was really my boss, but we were a very unique kind of partnership, because I had very different skills and we just sort of navigated it as the business needed different things."

While Carlene's husband was the CEO and visible leader to customers and suppliers on the outside, it was a different story inside the business. She acted as an internal peacemaker for a driven CEO who was sometimes insensitive to staff feelings. She listened to their concerns, took care of them, and created order where her husband was disorganized and over-promised.

When her husband died suddenly in mid-life, his mother and two sisters asked her to take over the business, and she did. She was really the only one capable of doing so. After his death, Carlene took on her husband's role as the mediator of family conflicts, continued to develop his dream, and created a platform for the next generation. Among her accomplishments was helping the competing family members divide the large business into parts and sell them to each other.

3

RAISING FAMILY STEWARDS

Besides their essential work in the family business, all the women we interviewed took on a second essential role: raising their children to be hard-working, respectful, and motivated. Even when the wife was her husband's helper or partner, the couple didn't share anything close to equal household roles. Indeed, the expectation in most of the families was the traditional one of the wife being responsible for the household and children, rather than continuing her own career or taking a defined leadership role with her husband. If she did work, it would be as a community volunteer. Even if household and work roles were divided, the women were expected to take on a dual role, with responsibility in both spheres.

In our research, we learned how these women amazingly managed the dual roles of business partner and primary parent by using soft power as the family's emotional steward or CEO (Chief Emotional Officer). One matriarch, who like her husband is also in the financial industry, observed: "The first-generation matriarch is a pivotal person in the life of the family and in the mental health of the children more than the entrepreneur. The entrepreneur can be a dictator or largely absent at home. If the matriarch is loving and accepting, those kids are okay. If the matriarch is judgmental and cold, those kids are screwed."

To some of these women, "having it all" seems to mean "doing it all." They said it can be exhausting taking on so many aspects of parenting while still supporting the grand vision of the business. One of them told us: "While my husband is working like crazy, all of the responsibilities of the family fell on my shoulders. And not just that, but managing the household, doing all the repairs, going to back-to-school nights, helping the kids with their homework, making sure they went to scouts, going to their ballgames, supporting them in their activities. And then also supporting [my husband] in his activities and trying to get him involved as a father in the family. ...If we wanted to involve him, we would have to go to work, make sure he was available. If we wanted a family portrait, we'd have to bring his clothes to him, maybe get a bit of dinner, take him back to work, and then go home and put the kids to bed."

> # To some of these women, "having it all" seems to mean "doing it all"—an exhausting effort of parenting and supporting the brand vision of the business.

Other women expressed frustration with the spouse's long hours and lack of time to devote to family. As a result, they tried to find creative ways to connect the children with their father. A few spouses said they actively intervened to overcome some of the founder's bad habits within the family, including this one: "My husband was a strong taskmaster, so sometimes I had to soften his influence on [our children] to be the best. ...A lot of time I was really bitter that he wasn't there to help me in the way I was supporting him. Later on, I realized when I watched our kids go into the business and see how they handled themselves and their responsibilities, I could see that a lot of what they learned came from him, even though he wasn't there all the time."

STORY 4:
Governance and Guidance for Future Generations

This woman charted a path for herself and her children in the family business. As those roles evolved, she focused on building structures that helped to develop cohesion and set up subsequent generations for success.

Grace, mother of five, and wife of an entrepreneur, never worked at the operating company, but always served as a sounding board to her husband. She was fully engaged in what was going on at her husband's company, while raising their children – and when needed, she would bring them in during the evenings to count inventory. Louis was very thoughtful about his business dealings and was committed to ensuring that the financing never left his family in a precarious situation. Grace shared that Louis used to say to the kids, "Don't ever put your lives at risk for money. Understand the value of it. Use it wisely. Use it for good things."

The two eldest started working at 12 and 14 years of age "doing really menial work. They had to work their way up." As they grew and earned the respect of business colleagues, it was other line managers who approached Louis to advocate for his kids. Preparing them was on Louis' mind as he moved into middle age. One day, he gathered his kids to the kitchen table and handed each of them a notebook and said, "you're going to want to take notes because I am going to teach you everything you need to know to run this business."

When Louis fell ill, Grace and her kids were on a solid footing with their businesses. And while her son became CEO, she stayed involved, just as her husband encouraged. She had unmatched institutional knowledge and experience. When conflict arose with her son, he stepped down and she began to concern herself with the longevity and management of the company. There was no board, and when Grace inserted herself to establish one, her kids were disappointed and felt judged. But through consistent family conversations and meetings, they came to understand the value and purpose of a corporate board. Years later, Grace established a family office to help her family become more cohesive and work together, especially with her grandchildren coming of age, and looking at the family enterprise as a possible future for them. Grace shared, "I don't know that they all take my advice, but I do think they're all good kids and they understand the value of wealth. The challenge is teaching it to their kids."

As with traditional couples that have complementary roles, several wives set aside their careers to focus on the family. One said: "I had two small children when I decided to leave [the business]. They were both just getting into elementary school. I wanted to be around for their childhood. The family business was growing well. I had been commuting a long distance to work for almost seven years and so I was ready to be home. ...I definitely was conscious of taking a step back career-wise to pretty much have more control of my time." Even during and after this shift, the wife was also able to help her husband grow the business.

The business and its success take dominant roles in these families, looming large in their lives as a passionate focus of one or both parents. We can only wonder what feelings their children have about this reality. How do they range between pride and reflected glory, and resentment and neglect? These conflicts are major themes in the life experience of next-generation offspring. They can accept the difficulties by looking at the benefits rather than the costs, or they can struggle and express frustration. One hallmark of these families is that the children come to share and take pride in the family connection to the business. But this wouldn't be the case without the active engagement of the wife or the widow in helping her kids develop those feelings.

One hallmark of these families is that the children come to share and take pride in the family connection to the business.

With the support and encouragement of their mothers, the children in these families become adults on their own life journeys, following one or more of three paths:

(1) working in the family business or acting as a board member;

(2) actively participating in family philanthropy; or

(3) pursuing separate professional careers while still helping with some aspects of the family enterprise.

Several of the next-generation family members we studied (three from the families of widows and two from two-parent families) have become leaders of the family enterprises. Other families have sold the business and either created a shared family office to handle investments or divided the payout to each family member. Two of the businesses became larger public companies with non-family leadership, although the family remains active in governance.

For many of the children, their major connection to the family enterprise comes from influence over money given to philanthropic causes. While the family can remain connected through these activities, they also start their own careers, mostly as professionals, to find their own way forward.

With our small sample of families, we cannot suggest any specific frequencies of successful outcomes among these paths, but there's a common theme: matriarchs use their role in the family to instill responsible values and extend a positive work ethic to their children. These women all take pride in having taught their children that, despite the family wealth, they're expected to work or be responsible for their family support; and their inheritance should supplement rather than support their lifestyle. While the children are wealthier and more fortunate than many of the women themselves were when they were growing up, they were taught the values of frugality, responsibility, hard work, and individual initiative—values that were not that dissimilar to those the mothers grew up with.

These mothers actively prepare their children for a positive future in five different ways:

1. Valuing relationships over recognition

The wife or life partner of the public-facing wealth creator carries out many activities to support and enable her spouse, all of them based on relationship. Through building trusting, caring, supportive relationships, the female family leader greatly influences and contributes to the family enterprise. Her relationships with her spouse, his parents and family, their children, company employees, and the community add value in many ways, some of which are not seen or given credit publicly. We can speculate that women live more by relationships and less by a narrow focus on achievements; and we can appreciate that this role is one of the foundations for a successful family enterprise.[12]

2. Raising active and engaged beneficiaries

It's common to hear wealthy parents fearing that their children will become spoiled and entitled by growing up with wealth. The women we interviewed shared that concern, but because of their own backgrounds and histories of working themselves as either creators or new owners of wealth, they actively encourage (maybe even pressure) their children to work when they're young. Of course, the most frequent place where they find employment is in the family enterprise. By working in the business (or in an entity such as a foundation or affiliated asset), growing children find satisfaction and learn to see themselves as contributors to the family, not just beneficiaries. They not only learn about the business but also see how other people work and maybe internalize that family members aren't too special to work.

A large percentage of the children eventually enter the family business—and in several families, all the siblings do so. Growing up alongside a family enterprise, many of the teenagers are called upon to help with business tasks, working after school, summers, and weekends. This isn't seen as a burden but rather an expectation—"this is what we do"—or it can be experienced as a special opportunity that allows them to see and work with their father in the work that he loves. They also feel pride in what they can contribute. As a result, they experience the business as an enterprise inviting them to take part, rather than as a distant, somewhat threatening force.

One of the women recounted how she urged her children to take summer jobs as teenagers. "I said to them, you aren't sitting around all summer," she said. "They always worked in the summer. I expected them to either have a job or work as a volunteer." Both of her sons now work for the business and are in line to become its new leaders.

Early employment may be a reason why so many of these families produce a next generation that chooses to work in the business. Since the business is an extension of the family, it's as natural to help out there as it is to help out at home. When the children spend time working in the business, the father goes from being a distant figure whose passion takes him away from the family to a figure who inspires and teaches them. But it's the mother's task to make this happen. By entering the spirit of the business, the children's connection diminishes any sense of feeling secondary to the business. And the distance between the father and kids shrinks—thanks to the mother.

3. Imparting family values and attitudes of gratitude

In what they taught and modeled for their children, the women were attentive to the values they held dear. One almost universal value seen in our study was frugality. Many women noted that although they were wealthy, their family lived well below its means and the children were taught not to expect or seek the most expensive items. All the women remembered a time when they weren't wealthy. They instilled attitudes of gratitude for what they had, along with a sense of humility. While entitlement and lavish lifestyles certainly existed, we heard that these families were proud that these weren't values they wanted or expected in their children. Women who grow up with an ethic of working hard and taking care of themselves didn't feel that these values were no longer needed. They understood that their success came from hard work, and they wanted their children to learn this same lesson.

After marrying into a sixth-generation family business, one woman saw that her husband's influence as the CEO was losing family support. So, she extended her professional expertise as a coach to get inside the head and even the heart of her husband's father—a global force in the food industry. She studied and wrote about the values, purpose, and meaning that the family stood for over the generations and how it earned respect by being able to honor the family legacy and tell it in a way that nurtured relationships and created family pride.

Another woman noted: "One of the things that I did after my husband passed was to articulate the values of the business we created, because I wanted to make sure we were all on the same page. That was a really difficult exercise, but it certainly helped in managing going forward and being the kind of leader that I was called to be."

4. Governing family through stories and solutions

Some of the women find that they're part of two different family entities. There's the elder family, which includes the husband's parents and siblings, along with their children or stepchildren and also his extended family—all of whom can be involved in the family enterprises. And there's her own family, with his children and their children as well as her extended family. These groups each may have a claim on the family wealth, and their complex relationships are a minefield of potential conflict.

The work of building a new generation includes much more than instilling a work ethic and attending to the values and skills of her children. Female family leaders want to have family conversations. They initiate family meetings, shared family activities, and family policies about decisions to organize the future and build cooperation within and across generations. They act as stewards by convening meetings to talk about what it means to be wealthy and what's the purpose of the wealth. Many families aren't comfortable talking about money; but the wealth-creators have a memory of not having wealth, or of families that had wealth but lost it. So, as part of teaching their children, they initiate family conversations about money and wealth.

The wives are often attuned to discussions about handling conflict and making decisions together—ones that are collaborative versus more one-sided. They're usually early adopters of the basic principles of family decision-making—or, as it's now more formally called, family governance. These women become mediators in conflict in their husband's family, using their position as the new family member to develop a role in which they're trusted to be fair and objective, rather than entering the conflict.

5. Encouraging their children to dream without limits

Only one of the women felt that her daughters had different career expectations than their sons. But they all felt that their daughters had the same chances as their sons to enter the family enterprise or be part of its governance; and of course, they all inherited equally. Overall, an equal number of sons and daughters entered the family enterprise.

Several mothers found that even though they may have been seen as taking on a traditional female role, they wanted to ensure that their daughters had an equal opportunity to follow their passion; and, in fact, they were encouraged to pursue careers. Also, they were careful to raise their sons to expect their sisters to be treated the same as them.

Nearly every woman mentioned some way in which they were active in challenging the traditional roles that often limited women's horizons. They wanted their daughters to know that their career and passion counted and should be respected. One said: "Women have to have the confidence to be able to contribute and have the will that both these things matter. It's a real choice. And if you have both then it's open to both... when you talk about work-life balance and raising a family. You can have it all, but I don't think you can have it all at the same time."

4

NAVIGATING WIDOWHOOD

The women in our study led truly exceptional lives, attaining wealth and success beyond their wildest expectations. They were in meaningful partnerships with their driven and influential husbands, and they produced wonderful children and families. But life can suddenly turn. Almost half of these first-generation female leaders eventually faced a stark development: the unexpected (and often sudden) death of their husbands. This traumatic, life-changing event redefined their roles in the family and in the family enterprise. They then faced a series of changes in widowhood: unexpected loss, stepping up, discovering an ability to lead with a different style than their husband's, and becoming a bridge for succession to the next generation.

Grief can be overwhelming when a close relationship ends. One woman spoke about being secluded at home for six months, utterly gripped with fear, until her mother-in-law, a deeply religious women, helped her deal with the anger and grief. She was persuaded that the business and her children needed her guidance. Another new widow required years of intensive therapy for severe depression, but she showed a brave face to the company and community. While personally burdened with sadness and grief, she took the reins of the business and turned it around—she felt many people counted on her.

From being behind the scenes and having business or financial demands placed on them (except for the ones they put on themselves), the widows were forced out from the shadows. Besides overcoming grief and loss, they had to tackle a challenging role and assume much greater responsibility. Often, their company was reeling, and it needed not just external leadership but also internal support for a workforce in pain and facing uncertainty. Throughout this turmoil, the widows had to show up and provide visible support to enable their businesses to continue.

Before one woman's husband died, he led a growing business with his mother and sister in a very closely connected family, with whom he had an often-contentious relationship. While he had a business background, neither the mother nor the sister had much education or experience, other than in the family business. His wife—who worked quietly on a few issues—valued his peacemaking ability and counseled him, but now she had to step up. After he died, she asked the others to get together for a family meeting when "the banks [were] asking, 'Who's going to be in charge here?' They all voted for me to run the business, and this was sort of logical, because I had been doing it with him for the past seven years. So, suddenly, boom, I was the president of the operating business."

As she took over the business, delaying her reaction to grief, she had to wade into interfamily conflict, finding that she needed to be more analytical and develop the peacemaking skills of her husband. His family were accustomed to his very informal leadership style, while she was more organized and formal. As a result, conflict emerged between the three family branches, and it became clear that, with their brother gone, they couldn't continue together. The widow engineered a sale of one division to her sister-in-law and divided another into several businesses, keeping the largest one for her branch of the family.

STORY 5:
Cementing a Legacy

A widow faced the task of not only continuing the family enterprise but also establishing the family legacy with a next generation.

Winona, who was considerably younger, lost her husband when he was nearly eighty after a thirty-five-year marriage. They had two young daughters, as well as an older son from her husband's first marriage. Both she and her husband came from wealthy families, but that wealth had been almost completely depleted before they married. Both were driven, type-A personalities, pushing for excellence, and both benefited from the perks of education and privilege. "You have connections, exposure and know how to act," Winona noted. As he developed his wealth through investment, she adopted a traditional role, raising their children and becoming active in the community with her background in music. "He couldn't have done what he did without a partner, and he was very cognizant of that."

After her husband had a stroke, they had two more years together before he died. His loss wasn't just personal. It affected the family's role in the community and how they were perceived. "You were living the dream; then all of a sudden you weren't any more," she said. "You're someone whose whole family had a tragic accident." She and her husband had been in the middle of raising funds for a huge philanthropic effort in their community, and she continued as a leader in these efforts. But her community role and power base were washed away.

Because she wasn't yet qualified to manage the wealth, Winona had to develop her finance skills. She continued working with her husband's advisors, but she learned to listen to her intuition and did the necessary research before making decisions. She began to feel that the advisors weren't coming to trust or respect her judgment. She started working with another financial advisor. And she still had a steep learning curve. "I was the new authority, and I probably was wearing the emperor's clothes," she said. "I deserve those clothes now. I earned them."

Her young daughters grew up like she did, knowing they were wealthy but training in values such as work and frugality. She gave them some money to manage while they were in college and brought them into both the financial and philanthropic affairs of the family. Also, she has actively taught them and encouraged them to become active in their community. She didn't want her daughters to emerge as unprepared as she had once felt.

5

REMARRIAGE AND STEPFAMILIES

The traditional nuclear family is no longer a given today. With longer life expectancy and emphasis on personal satisfaction as an expectation of a good marriage, affluent parents often have more than one marriage. A "blended" family is one in which at least one partner is divorced, with children from an earlier marriage; and so there can be a connection with a former spouse. And young children can be faced with a new parent living in their household or claiming the attention of their custodial parent.

Second marriages are rife for conflict in how family wealth is inherited and can spark painful rifts or family feuds. We interviewed several spouses who married successful wealth creators. They were mindful of the precarious nature of their status in the family and often took active steps to anticipate and avoid negativity and create harmony in the extended family.

Several of the women married business creators with children from an earlier marriage; they were often new to the level of wealth in their new family. There's no defined role for a "second wife" and there's a good chance that she may invite conflict with the rest of the family. The new spouse can be considerably younger and be seen as a competitor or intruder by the children—the more so, the older they are. The new spouses in our study didn't want to remain disconnected from their new stepchildren or act as a distant rival for their father's affection. They defined positive, distinctive contributing roles to the business and the family that avoided or overcame conflict. In each family, the new wife understood the potential for conflict and so she actively reached out not only to connect with the stepchildren but also with her new husband's former wife.

STORY 6:
The "Force Multiplier"

The new wife of a man who has created a large family business and has his own grown children can be quite a challenge. This woman succeeded by developing a unique and unexpected matriarchal role.

Meryl married late to a business leader. Each of them came with grown children. She saw herself as a "force multiplier" who could use little things to make a big difference in all their lives. She and her kids joined a business family split by a contentious divorce, and so one of her goals was to create harmony in the family. She did that by reaching out to the former wife, the mother of his children, to include her in family activities. The plan succeeded, greatly reducing family tension, and even allowing them to share family holidays.

Meryl also undertook several projects to build the family culture and connect the family. She wrote a history of the company, highlighting the contributions of many family members, including that of her husband and his former wife. Then she followed up by starting a monthly family newsletter. Each issue interviewed a family member. She told us how this developed: "My husband's late-in-life goal was to be close to his family. He focused on the first thing that he wanted [after his divorce and new marriage], which was to heal a rift that was tearing the family apart. Next, he always wanted to communicate values to his children because he felt they were the secret to a happy life. If you have admirable values like honesty and reliability, you have a much better chance of having friends, having respect, getting good jobs. He wanted to communicate this to his children and to those who came after him, but he wasn't sure how to do it.

"My father used to have what he called 'family hour' in which he would just lecture at us—but that wasn't my husband's personality. He couldn't see himself standing up in front of his children for an hour every Sunday and lecturing at them after church services. So, we came up with another idea, which has just been so powerful and useful and satisfying. I said, 'What if I write a newsletter in which I interview you about things that you consider important like prenups or being frugal or caring about where you came from?'

"It was a full-page newsletter that would come out by mail once a month. Each family member would get their own copy. The day the newsletter arrived, everybody would drop everything, tear it open, and read it, and then they'd talk about it. That was pretty satisfying for me—getting feedback that they loved it.

"It began to branch out so that I wouldn't just interview my husband. I interviewed aunts and uncles. I told stories from way back. Like times with the company where there was a crisis, and they could have gone bankrupt—the terrible problems as well as the magnificent successes."

She said that the newsletter has evolved not just to share family experiences but also for family members to respond to deep questions like "What does it mean to be me?" *or* "Who's your greatest hero?"

Meryl did not stop there. She created whole family vacations every year as a way for different generations to get together and to know and value each other. These connections have led to a real community among the now several generations of family members. And after the passing of her husband, these activities have kept the family connected. She's now regarded as the elder in the family, preparing to pass family leadership to a daughter in the next generation.

This was Meryl's way of being the family's "chief emotional officer" as she called it. She created an ongoing, engaged cross-generational family community that mirrored the values and work ethic of the company's patriarch. As the family storyteller, she was extraordinary at "managing the family story" and ensuring that its reputation is now honored and protected.

Another woman we interviewed said she married later in life when both her own and his kids were nearly grown. Her new husband was already a revered leader in the company, while she began to add another dimension. He held many values on employee engagement and community, but she saw that they weren't being fully expressed or implemented. She had a more human, personal touch. So, she began to work on these activities, building on the values framework of the patriarch and adding her own much more open and expressive style to create opportunities to build community within the company. As a result, the company culture became more aligned with its values, as well as more open and collaborative. This is how she described her work: "The matriarch's role is transmission of values across generations. Part of that is education and the importance of doing well and being motivated—earning things, not being given things for the reason of being wealthy. I think the major role is to steer, to see things, and be attracted to them, but learn to set your own path. ...The transition of values is definitely a partnership and requires teamwork."

The above examples show that new wives can shift the tenor of the family, build or sustain family connection, and act as mentors to their new children. They define and differentiate their role by being available to help their children and stepchildren, especially girls, make decisions and formulate their lives. In two of the families we studied, the new mother helped her stepdaughters enter the business and take on leadership roles. Another wife adopted a traditional role in her marriage, but was a leader in the community, working with her husband in a huge community philanthropic enterprise. Because of her leadership, she was able to bring her children into that activity as well, and their roles grew after her husband's death.

STORY 7:
Fostering Family Unity

Marrying into a family of wealth may open a new life, especially if it's a second marriage for a single mother. This is the story of a woman who married into a family of old wealth that was growing apart, and, through her leadership, took his blended family on an independent path.

Ginny made a commitment to her husband, but she wasn't prepared to relate to a family that grew up with incredible wealth. Her role was to help her husband forge his own separate path and raise children to follow their own values, not those of their extended family. Her husband, Jerry, had grown up wealthy but lived a simple life and didn't think of himself as wealthy, even if he knew that was the case.

When she met Jerry, Ginny was raising her four children as a single mother. In their first conversation at a party, she had no idea of his lineage. He began to spend time at her house, and they got to know each other as their relationship progressed. She learned of his legacy but neither of them spent much time thinking about his wealth. It wasn't a topic that was really discussed in his family. Jerry was a trustee of a large trust fund, but he lived a frugal, quiet life as a furniture maker. Like Ginny, he cared deeply about nature and art, and they wanted to create their own path. So, her role in getting them to differentiate from the extended family was crucial.

Here's how she described their relationship: "I don't know if it's old-fashioned, but we clung to our intentional ignorance and just thought we could see if we could make a life together. ...My job is to be his helpmate. We were very close, spent a huge amount of time together. I have long gone to all his trust meetings. We do Zoom meetings and review things together. We're involved in our foundation and choose charitable activities that we value together. We enable each other, hopefully in a good way, to be more forward and complete people. ...I'm a cheerleader for Jerry. He has a lot of complicated financial responsibilities that are slightly invisible, and I stand with him on those."

With a shared ignorance and disinterest in the family wealth, Ginny and her four children moved to his estate. Her kids were a little overwhelmed at first, but they didn't talk about it. Jerry and Ginny soon had two children together and he adopted her kids—and they agreed to treat all six of them equally. They shared personal values they wanted to leave pass to their children. "[We are] aspirationally high-minded for what really will work and be good in our culture and be good on our planet. I don't mean to sound too grandiose but that's a big deal for us."

Ginny became the originator and driver of family conversations and meetings in their own growing family to live sustainably. After attending a family wealth seminar, they began to talk about the purpose of their family trust, discovering the need for conversations in the extended family about the future of their wealth. As their children grew up, the family meetings focused on educating the children about their wealth and talking about social values and philanthropy. After a cautious, sometimes reluctant start, the family began to enjoy these meetings and learn to communicate more openly.

By bringing these ideas into Jerry's extended family, they were not trying to challenge the family but just follow ideas they thought were sensible. Even though Jerry wasn't close with his siblings or divorced parents, they spent time at his family's vacation place. The meetings were helpful, but the conversations petered out as their financial holdings became less interconnected. "I tried to just keep it going, not give up," Ginny said. "If somebody is not interested in your meeting, that doesn't matter. You can just try to make it more interesting. But you're not going to pack your bags and go home because it's frustrating or you don't have 100 percent buy-in." She felt she had some influence on the extended family, but their focus was with their own children and eventually she let go of her attempt to bond the extended family and instead recommitted her efforts to her own family.

"With our kids there are subtle struggles and conflicts, and we try to resolve them. I think we were called 'laissez-faire' parents," she said. "We have high expectations but a long timeline. ...I'm hoping that our laissez-faire parenting will make them more resilient and adaptable and that their gratitude for the life they're offered will carry them forward to be constructive and sharing as they continue in their lives."

Their kids became very active in social projects—like starting a sustainable elementary school. Now they have grandchildren, ages twelve to twenty-three, and they're also included in education and family meetings. Together, Ginny and Jerry are looking deeply at their values and are working together on personal development for each of them. She believes that inherited wealth isn't shameful or something to hide. It can do a lot of good. "I have the role with my own [children and grandchildren] to encourage the multilayers of education and things that have to do with their place in the community," she said. "You can't help with your place in the community if you can't help yourself; and the way to do it is by trying to learn and grow to be your best self. ...They've been raised to understand it's not enough to value work but that it's important in our culture for your work to reflect more."

Their children didn't have to consider working for money, but their grandchildren do, as their inheritance is lower. It's a challenging dynamic to navigate. "The next generation is being given a slightly different message," Ginny concluded. "That they should [both] be earners and choose something that does good in the world."

THE VARIOUS ROLES OF FIRST-GENERATION WOMEN

Wives of first-generation wealth creators engineer a pioneering, complex role that adds immense, if not always obvious, value to the long-term success of the family enterprise. Their contributions can be as impactful and consequential as those of the business founder. Husband and wife both contribute to the enterprise and become architects in the stewardship and development of the successor generation.

As our female pioneers imagined their future, they drew on their enormous experience managing multiple aspects of the family enterprise, including support of their husbands, development of their children, community engagement, and formal (or often hidden, informal) roles in the business and family finances. They overcame and worked past gender stereotypes and bias, not clamoring for better policies or external forces to help pave their way. Instead, they dug deep within themselves to identify what they wanted for the future of their family and how they could be a bridge. They also wanted to ensure the kind of change they sought for the next generation. They lived through their own crises of confidence and fears and saw not only how wealth can have negative impacts but also how their own wisdom and foresight led them to believe and succeed.

The wife's role takes many forms as it evolves from the early days of business creation to the growth and development of a capable and contributing rising generation. Life-cycle issues, including death or divorce, offer further challenges to the business and family future. As we've seen, the women in these families take on several roles:

- **Essential business partner and contributor**: The spouse often doesn't expect to have a role, but whether intentional or not, she takes on a key task that makes it possible for the business to prosper. Her contribution is often not recognized or visible.

- **Multi-generational steward of family business and legacy**: The family grows up with unexpected wealth and has an implicit obligation to build upon what has been started. The wife sees the impact of the husband's focus on the business and so she attends to the needs of the sons and daughters, connecting them to the business and helping them prepare for roles as stewards of the family legacy.

- **Pioneer building meritocratic gender awareness**: The spouse wants to continue as a role pioneer and sustain her daughters and sons by giving them an unrestricted view of gender roles and opportunities for family leadership.

- **Purveyor of family culture and values**: As the family becomes wealthy and faces questions about what they want to do with their wealth and enterprise, the new matriarch takes the lead in bringing the family together to make these choices. They teach values about life to their children and are role models for responsible behavior, setting clear expectations for succession.

THE JOURNEY OF THE NEW MATRIARCH

Several common themes emerged from the experience of these wise first-generation women that define a path that is essential to the success of the family. These qualities are the essence of what it means to be "self-made." While we'll see some of these qualities echoed in the stories of later generation women family leaders, they faced the added challenge of having few if any preexisting role models for their achievement:

- **No preparation**: Few of them felt prepared or had formal training; traditionalism, gender stereotyping, and unconscious bias played a role here.

- **Inner drive and confidence:** These women were open to learning and had an inner sense of confidence in themselves and an ability that was fostered in their upbringing.

- **Supportive husband:** Those most successful at emerging as co-creators and leaders had husbands who were open to treating them as partners and confidantes.

- **Alone, but not lonely:** They felt alone in their journeys, other than the company of their spouses, but they weren't necessarily lonely.

- **No leadership awareness:** They rarely saw themselves as leaders, but on behalf of their families, they just kept putting "one foot in front of the other."

- **Filled a gap:** Their initial involvement almost always was due to some kind of "gap"—a death, a need to make money to support the family, or a love of a needy spouse—and they stepped in just because something "had to be done."

- **Mediator between spouse and family:** They mediated between their entrepreneur/husband, children, and extended family, building communication, connection, and collaboration.

- **Drive children's development:** They supported and encouraged their children's development of business and life skills, especially those of their daughters or daughters-in-law, establishing a strong education commitment.

As we begin to see how a new generation of millennial couples define their roles together, there are signs that the changes we're seeing will continue. It may be that millennials—with whom there is gender equality in education and in starting business and professional roles—may be more likely to move toward "copreneurial" roles rather than the complementary roles that we've learned about. And there are signs that in parenting and family, men are tending toward more egalitarian roles, by doing such things as cooking and paying more attention to their place in the family.

PART II
inheritors
of wealth

6

THE COMPLEX FAMILY LEADERSHIP ROLE OF WOMEN INHERITORS

We've seen the creative and influential roles of new matriarchs in the success of their family enterprise. But many business families don't have such women role models of assertion and active influence to prepare rising-generation women in their families for active leadership. Women come from successful families where women have not been active leaders and where traditional patriarchal values predominate. These young women emerge in a social environment where women have begun to ask for more equality and they face a family environment that has not yet come to this place. These women are inheritors and beneficiaries of family wealth, but they feel called upon to create change within their families. Since they didn't have the benefit of a new matriarch in their families, these successors have to become pioneers in their families to define a more egalitarian and collaborative role for women. This section defines the path of another type of new matriarch, a woman who comes from a traditional family business culture who exercises power and influence as a successor. While the women successors have some qualities similar to the first-generation matriarchs, the role and experience of successor women leaders is different enough to merit separate treatment, even though there will be echoes of the previous section in their stories.

Although women are on track to inherit a major share of wealth over the coming years, the women we interviewed rarely began with direct influence over their inherited wealth—which is often controlled by trustees or men in the family. Even when they do have control, women inheritors can be tentative, lack confidence in their decisions and authority, or downplay their influence. Since they don't expect to be responsible for the wealth, they may disregard getting prepared or educated on the subject. But because they see that wealth has implications on their and their family's health and wellbeing, women heirs are increasingly taking an active leadership role in their family's wealth.

In what way does family wealth need leadership? Many families become wealthy by starting and sustaining successful family businesses, and many of the women in our study become family business leaders. But family wealth takes more forms than a single company. By the second generation, the families may sell their legacy business or invest the profits in other ventures and assets—ranging from family vacation homes and real estate to family offices with extensive financial portfolios. They also "invest" in philanthropy and social ventures. To maintain these diverse assets and sustain the extended family's identity, it needs several kinds of leadership. This diversity leads us to the term "family enterprise" when referring to family assets that consist of more than a single business. And the rising-generation families these women lead represent diversified portfolios and can include a family office and a foundation, rather than legacy businesses.

Family wealth takes different forms by the second and later generations, and over half of these families had sold the legacy business or seen the family business take its place as one asset among many. And most of the families had a family office that managed their wealth, even in cases where the family had major ownership of a business.

The family needs more than one leader for these multiple generations and ventures and, as we'll see, the leadership of rising-generation women takes many forms. Increasingly, women occupy key positions, but their ascension can be choppy, because they must challenge family traditions, including patriarchy, and redefine what's possible for women.

We interviewed nineteen female family heirs who became leaders in their family enterprises and wealth management. They ranged in age from their late forties to the eighties, with an average age in the mid-sixties. Most of them had children and some also had grandchildren, so we were able to learn about their roles in the family and in the business. Half the women we talked to led their family businesses, while the other half achieved leadership within a more diversified family enterprise.

Most of the women heirs had professional skills and careers either before or while they were taking on roles in the family enterprise. But becoming a female leader in a multi-generation family enterprise is often a new role, one with few precedents or role models for women. To succeed, the female heir must be confident, capable, and prepared, while at the same time defining these new leadership roles.

Becoming a female leader in a multi-generational family enterprise is often a new role, one with few precedents or role models for women.

In this second part of our study, we explore how they came into the role of family leader and in what form; how they balance work and family responsibilities; and how they collaborate with their parents, siblings, children, and advisors. Their experience forces us to take a broader view of the nature of family wealth and enterprise leadership and the extraordinary contributions made by these women. This chapter considers the complex family leadership role of women inheritors. Later chapters present four phases of the circuitous journey to leadership, establishing family governance to create a shared future, and leveraging experiences to bridge to the future.

This is a new era for female leadership in the family and its multiple enterprise structures. Our study explores the evolution and experience of women inheritors who have moved beyond traditional female roles and achieved leadership and responsibility for the family enterprises that hold the wealth. While families today increasingly view their daughters as potential successors, the daughters are still burdened by the residue of a social environment in which women were not considered available, capable, or on par with men. So, women's path to family leadership is more improvisational, complicated, and challenging than that of their brothers.

Their growing engagement in family leadership includes more than managing financial wealth. These women see leadership as having to do with the "relationships" between the senior generations and their siblings, and the raising and educating of their children. These women leaders are also responsible in the more traditional role as the family "caretaker," maintaining its culture and raising productive children. These inheritors, like their first-generation mothers, combine the responsibilities of work, financial, and family matters.

They become family leaders by creating a family culture that brings the old and new generations together to use their wealth wisely and productively. They do this in a way that we believe takes a different, more expansive form, because of their gender. These women have become "family culture innovators." We cannot say that this role is played only by women, but we observe that many women in families of wealth play this role as the family crosses generations. They told us they feel that they had no choice but to modernize the family culture. Their parents were raised in an earlier generation, so if the family were to offer opportunities to them as daughters, the culture had to change so that their own children would not face the same obstacles.

These women were forced to modernize the family culture, born of parents raised in an earlier generation constrained by predated societal norms.

We were inspired by how they imagined their new roles, often by challenging traditional standards, and found ways to transform the family without generating acrimony or conflict. They were able to let go of past mistakes and frustrations, forgive family members, and have the courage to stand up for the changes they felt were necessary. They became especially active as the family built paths toward more active communication, meetings, and family events. Acting on social values and goals, they became more open and egalitarian in requests for active service from all members of the family, not just the business leaders.

This social evolution doesn't have a clear beginning and end; it's a winding road with many twists and turns. For these women, taking leadership wasn't a single event entering an established role. Inspired by their vision and overcoming many obstacles, the women accumulated influence and leadership of the family. They were both beneficiaries and change leaders in fostering gender equality and establishing a family enterprise in which merit and capability replaced hereditary status. We conceptualize this as a series of steps as these women moved into various leadership roles in the family and the business world until they fully found their voice. They then prepared their children to move into this new role.

The women we interviewed have become major players in the transition and evolution of the woman's role in family, career, and wealth. Their stories don't have an ultimate destination. They chronicle the challenges that arise when growing up in a period of social ferment and changing roles. They've become social entrepreneurs as well as family leaders, taking them in new directions.

STORY 8:
Serving as Family Diplomat

To give some context to the pioneering woman's emerging role, this account illustrates the delicacy and dynamics of her journey toward leadership. While rising-generation women are not immediately perceived as potential leaders or successors, several of those we interviewed said that their emotional intelligence and family diplomacy led to their successful leadership in the family and the business.

Nora is the oldest of four siblings in the third generation of a large service-industry business. They were raised together and working in the family business became "part of their DNA." It was a totally male-dominated business, so Nora didn't initially consider working there herself. However, because that industry was the only one that she knew, she found herself working in a similar business. To everyone's surprise except her own, she did very well—and she liked it, becoming a sales leader and a great performer. Two of her brothers had entered the family business, and after a while she and her husband were asked to work at one of its company offices. Nora excelled once more, even while she raised their two children. The whole family was close, with many family members working in various roles, and they began having family meetings.

Nora, rather than the two brothers, was selected to lead the business because of her ability to deal directly, but caringly, with delicate topics. Her confidence also meant she had no hesitation about entering this previously all-male world. "I had taken leadership roles early on with our family meetings and we've been talking about succession and what was going to happen," she said. "I had been successful in almost everything I touched. I had been active in the community. I started out as a member of a group and before I knew it, ended up heading it."

The family had an outside board of advisors, but her father, at eighty-eight, was still in charge. She became co-chair with him, but there were tensions between them when her father resisted stepping down. So, she had to deliver the news to him in a delicate and respectful manner: "He left sadly but understood." None of her brothers could have accomplished this without deep bad blood.

Nora led the company in overcoming several additional challenges. They had an attractive buy-out offer, but as a family they decided not to accept it. Their longtime non-family CEO wanted to retire, and they had several internal candidates, including her husband. He didn't get the job, and they selected another non-family successor, a transition she had to lead through despite the personal ramifications to her marriage. "I don't see myself as a woman. I see myself as the leader," she said. To her, leadership is not connected to gender, a view shared by several of the younger inheritors.

To put this new role and the path to it for rising generation inheritors in context, we consider three topics:

1. Ensuring the positive impact of a growing fortune

As enormous wealth flows across generations, inheritance can be experienced as a mixed blessing. How does this windfall affect their future? What do they do with their wealth? When women emerge as the leaders, they must decide with their families how their wealth will affect them as individuals, as a family, as a group of enterprises, and within their community. A large inheritance can be more of a responsibility, even a burden, than a gift. While it can provide freedom and open possibilities for a comfortable life, it can also be connected to navigating a family through difficult circumstances with a portfolio of business and financial enterprises. So, to preserve wealth for future generations, family stewards must attend to sustaining and adding to the assets, as well as monitoring wealth's effect on the family.

It may be enormous, but wealth must be managed and nurtured. Its presence can trigger conflict in the family, and the steward must decide how it can and should be used, how it fits into the family, who gets what, who's involved in decision-making, and how it affects family relationships. As wealth passes across generations, the leaders must be responsible and effective in safeguarding the wealth while promoting positive family relationships. Traditionally, the presence of trustees and patriarchy meant that inheritors rarely had to develop their own skills. Now the inheritors, both male and female, share the responsibilities along with the benefits.

As the amount of wealth grows, so do the demands of leadership. Leaders must support and sustain a family culture that encourages responsible behavior and the contribution of next-generation family members. While, traditionally, men had a much larger share of the responsibility, today women are increasingly taking on these leadership roles.

2. Defining new roles for women in 'old money' families

Several of the women we interviewed come from families with several generations of wealth. Most of them have sold their legacy family business and become family enterprises, with a family office, shared real estate, and a family foundation. These "old money cultures" are defined by tradition, which these women often challenged or redefined. They had to be disruptors, innovators, and sometimes healers.

The extended family is a dominating force in the lives of these women. Each new generation brings increased complexity of branches, households, locations, values, and needs that strains the limits of the traditional structure. Role change is a social and political topic—such as women's suffrage, co-education, and entry into formerly gender-segregated careers. But the actions of these female leaders show how a "trend" can move from societal opportunity to family reality. These women are the true pioneers, plucking and building upon social trends to create cultural change in the longstanding norms of their own families. We believe that women inheritors who have experienced the impact of wealth have the wisdom to see around the corner in a way that those who are new to wealth don't have. They've experienced pain and blessings, and they use that knowledge to prepare their children and grandchildren in a very intentional way.

Sometimes, they departed from the family for their own path, not returning as a family enterprise leader. But their example of willingness to move on could be a force in their families; that divergent role was itself a significant departure from family tradition. They were then seen as family leaders, rising to the level of pioneers, in changing the family culture to offer more opportunity to themselves, their daughters, and their sons.

3. Reshaping traditional dynamics in families and family businesses

Every family, regardless of culture, begins with the biological realities of gender and birth order. Traditionally, there were clear differences in what a man and a woman were allowed to do. Men were assigned to business roles and authority, women to housework and childrearing. When women did work outside the home, they were given "pink-collar" roles—such as nursing, teaching, administrative, and social work.

Men and women were also expected to take different roles in relation to family wealth. Men became the stewards and managers, creating additional wealth; and while women could benefit from the wealth, they were expected to allow the male family leaders to take care of them. But over the past hundred years, the roles have shifted in the direction of greater balance, choice, and fluidity.

Also, there were social restrictions about marriage. When they married, women were expected to leave their family of origin and join her spouse's family. Husbands controlled the wealth, while the wives budgeted for the household. Their different roles offered order and predictability to social life, but they were also a constraint and source of frustration—as we read in the novels of Jane Austen and other nineteenth century authors. Today, there's a clear trend of more fluidity and even equality in spousal roles, especially when it comes to women having access to education and careers. The old subordinate roles have been largely rejected as women discover they can assume ones that require skill and offer power and responsibility.

In families where fathers or male siblings hold a less open, even unwelcomed view of the new order, this evolution can be a source of conflict. Added to that, a patriarch can present himself as being open to women entering traditional male roles, but he may unconsciously take actions that reflect the old ways. One daughter observed, "My father was traditional about the household but flexible in the business." This is the family of the unequal playing field that most women in our study entered.

Other parts of family structure that are always present include birth order and family hierarchy. The family isn't deemed a democracy. The older siblings loom large over their younger counterparts and tend to have greater power and authority due to their gender and age. The family hierarchy is a formative reality for every sibling. Feelings and relationships born of that hierarchy never leave. A younger sister or older brother will always retain aspects of childhood roles with siblings, a reality that the world may never be aware of. The dominant sibling could be a caring and benevolent leader but could also be controlling, intimidating, and intolerant. The challenge for the family is to develop business and financial leadership that works best for all members.

When there's a difference between the family and business hierarchies—with different leaders—conflict can emerge, and perhaps its origin is not clearly seen by the participants. That was the case in a classic article[13] in which the oldest son was the expected successor in the family hierarchy, while the daughter led the business. The family hierarchy can also be disrupted by a woman taking a formal leadership role in the business. The reality today is that the most capable leader may not be the one that follows the traditional order of gender and birth. And different generations can be at different stages of openness and evolution in how they see the woman's role, how they expect their daughters to act, and what roles they expect them to occupy.

7 ELEMENTS OF TRADITIONAL FAMILY CULTURES

The female wealth inheritors in this study described traditional wealthy family cultures as having several common features that they faced and challenged:

- **Well-defined family:** A culture with traditions, rituals, shared family homes, vacations, and many unspoken rules.

- **Frugality values:** A lifestyle preserving family wealth.

- **Traditional roles:** A clearly defined hierarchy with a strong family leader, usually a patriarch, though in some families, the role was taken by an elder matriarch, often the widow of a patriarch.

- **Secrecy about wealth:** An avoidance of direct conversations about money and a lifestyle hiding wealth in public.

- **Hidden alliances:** Unspoken personal agendas on preference and advancement of family branches and potential leaders.

- **Growing wealth dependency:** Family members pursue their personal careers and directions with the continued support of family wealth and status.

- **Marriage to achieve power:** Women are subordinate in a marriage, can have status in the community and with family, but not in business. You get status from whom you marry.

7

FOUR STAGES OF THE CIRCUITOUS JOURNEY TO LEADERSHIP

Half of our rising generation of pioneer women became family enterprise CEOs—as the formal leaders of the family business or family office. The other half became less-visible leaders (in their family office or financial affairs). Succession is an issue for every family enterprise, but for women it appears that the road is far more circuitous and complex. Patriarchy is a tradition in the family business, not only for parents and perhaps siblings but also for employees and the business community. Tradition doesn't shift easily. So, women leaders cannot assume they'll be embraced as legitimate leaders, even if their professional skills make them appropriate, suitable, and more than capable.

The succession process into leadership for either gender is a progression of steps that begin with introducing a young family member to the family enterprise. But women face complexity and resistance that males do not. We look here at the stages that define succession for the women inheritors in our study:

STAGE 1: MAKING THE CHOICE TO CHALLENGE THE ESTABLISHED CULTURE

Typically, women grow up with few if any role models of female leadership inside or outside the family. Yet the ones in our study did not seem to absorb a woman's secondary role. Three striking themes emerge from the stories of their upbringing, that echo the experience of the first-generation women we profiled in the previous chapter:

- **Strong bonds with their fathers:** Some of the women noted that they didn't have a brother to take the dominant role, or that their personal assertiveness and energy caught their father's attention. For whatever reason, their fathers understood their nature and didn't treat them as ornamental, delicate, or passive daughters. From early on, the daughters knew that they were capable of taking on more influential roles than women in the family took previously, and they felt that they had the support of their fathers.

Fathers realize early their daughters' talent and capability, but they're often surprised by their interest in becoming leaders. The women we interviewed say they were met with a somewhat positive if bemused reception from the patriarch, who hadn't considered them in that role before. If a father does see their success in outside careers, he's more open, maybe, than he was before. His role is clearly critical at this point—if he's not receptive, then his daughter may lose interest and the family may lose a talent. The father who comes from the traditional concept of a woman's role must be open to change and overcome the usual male dominance in the family. If he supports her, it enhances, prepares, and supports her future success.

- **A strong sense of self:** Personal drive was an influential role in their lives, that often ran contrary from the family tradition. Confident in their own abilities, they didn't allow themselves to be slotted into the typical women's roles. They discovered new directions, often as pioneers. When the family didn't offer them a positive role, they were ready, even willing, to go off on their own and develop their skills. Often, after a few years of travel and professional growth, they were able to negotiate re-entry to the family enterprise for a position of real leadership as an agent of changing family culture.

- **Education as an important step:** The women who would become family leaders studied business as undergraduates or at the graduate level. Seeing emerging opportunities, they wanted to be ready to pursue them. In a departure from family history, one woman was the first in her six-generation family to finish college. Females in these social strata were encouraged to study liberal arts, as one woman noted, "to become an interesting dinner partner."

The journey of self-development usually took an indirect path. Several viewed their marriage to a strong person (maybe similar to their father) as an initial step to self-realization. Sometimes they pursued a parallel career, but when they began to have kids, the traditional expectation prevailed, and they stepped off the career ladder. They later found the call of the family enterprise a surprise.

> # From tentatively stepping foot onto the career ladder, to stepping off to raise their children, these women's journeys of self-development were circuitous and complex.

Most rising-generation women begin their careers outside the family orbit, unlike men, who are often seen as a potential successor early in their lives. Since the females don't start out with a dream of succession, they pursue a separate career and often follow their husbands to another location. Perhaps a family crisis or a personal life change (such as a divorce or death in the family) leads them to take another look at the family business or larger family enterprise structure. And because of their life experience, careers, and maturity, they're comfortable and confident to initiate the process of returning to the family and entering the family enterprise.

STORY 9:
A Path from Old Money

Carey comes from a family that has been prosperous for six generations and has many sources of family wealth. Her story, beginning with inner development, illustrates the journey from wealth to leadership.

Carey grew up in an enclave where everyone was wealthy, and so she had no idea that this was unusual or special. She may have heard some things but said that until she was eighteen, she had no real idea of her family's wealth. Paradoxically, when she was informed of her trust fund and inheritance, she was upset. "I guess I was angry because it made me different," she said, "and it made me feel like I have to work extra hard to be recognized for my own abilities. People would just say, 'Oh, she got that because they have money.' So, I became determined to excel at whatever I was doing in spite of the background of wealth and also not telling anyone about it."

Education was not something that women were expected to pursue. She recalled a conversation with her grandfather: "He asked me, 'What in the world do you want all that education for? You're just going to get married and have babies.' I was in the back seat of the car behind him. He was driving. If he hadn't been driving, and if I had had something in my hand, I would have hit him, I was so angry. I just saw red. With that, I very calmly said, 'Fine. You don't have to pay for it. I'll pay for it myself,' and so I did."

Carey went off on her own, working in a place where she and her family weren't known. She wanted to be "a normal person, not be someone that people looked at and thought, 'Oh well, she's got an easy life.' It took several years on my own to finish off that process of not being angry, being positive, wanting to live my own life the way I wanted to live it, not the way my domineering mother wanted me to live it."

She married a businessman who didn't come from great wealth, and they had children. She became comfortable using her wealth to enhance her life and educate her children, and she became active in community affairs. She developed into a community leader, taking on some big projects that had visible success, and she was noted for her capability. Her brother ran the family office and wasn't making good financial decisions. When their mother died, she was asked to become trustee of the family trust, replacing her brother as family financial leader. Carey has also raised her daughters to become financially capable, independent, and responsible.

Pursuing parallel careers with their husbands may not lead to similar paths for spouses even though they have similar credentials. Being treated differently because of gender can lead to pressure to slip into traditional roles. For example, one woman who grew up comfortably and pursued the difficult path of becoming a surgeon, faced opposition from both her mother and her new profession. Her mother was firm that a woman need not work, let alone pursue a career or passion. In fact, her mother warned her daughter that her fiancé, also a newly trained surgeon, was only interested in her for her money. When she repeated her mother's fears to her fiancé, he assured her of his love, and said she would always manage his salary as a world-renowned surgeon; and to this day, that's true. She too became a surgeon and viewed her work as her calling. Through sheer grit and determination, she worked hard to earn her place in the field as an equal partner with her husband. But her journey was very different from her husband's much smoother one.

Another way to shed traditional expectations can come through divorce. Although some daughters' lives are uprooted when they divorce, for others it turns out to be a developmental step. One woman, who started her career at a financial institution and whose husband had a hugely successful career, assumed that "when your husband is making all the money, you sort of feel like, it's his money." Therefore, she felt she was unentitled to share his wealth. Their divorce drove her to pay more attention to her own means, which now came from two sources: her family and her husband. To educate herself about her wealth, she began to work in her family office, seeking advisors who would respect her and support her natural intellectual curiosity and interest. They helped affirm her conviction to being comfortable and knowing what she knows and what she doesn't know. She now stays very informed and concerns herself with making sure that her daughters don't adopt the same passivity she had as they lead their own lives.

For some women, divorce uprooted their lives and harmed traditional familial expectations, but for others, it turned into a step of self-discovery and growth.

On their own again, several divorced family heirs we interviewed experienced awakenings. Some began to listen to their own inner guides, developing careers and work that reflected their own values and interests. For example, one became a life coach and developed programs for women to find their own path; others became non-profit community leaders. They also focused on their own families or extended families, creating programs for family engagement.

One of their goals was to help young people become more conscious of their opportunities and more engaged in building their own relationships within the family and charting a future for them all. The women's view was that the lack of attention to whom they were as a family of wealth was leading the rising generation into a dangerous passivity that threatened their own future and the family legacy, as well as their own personal happiness and fulfillment. They become active mentors to young family members, including their own children, setting up educational and development-oriented family gatherings, and defining a culture that openly and directly expresses the values and mission of their extended family.

STAGE 2: ENTERING THE FAMILY ENTERPRISE

Rising-generation women described several entry routes to the family enterprise. Some felt called by the family to take the burden of responsibility. However, importantly, they did so on their terms. For example, one demanded her father name her CEO or she would leave, knowing that neither of her siblings were skilled or willing enough to take the job. Another had no male siblings, so she was the only one available. Another, in order to become independent of her less-interested siblings, had to buy the business from her dad.

STORY 10:
Facing Difficulties and Advantages

While the talented son of a family that owns a business might be expected to enter the business and become the successor, a woman's path to leadership is more problematic, as she faces gentle winds of traditional expectations.

Arlene's father owned a bank, but she grew up not knowing much about the business or even that the family had wealth. She learned lessons from her family about frugality because they gave her a bank account in middle school. Her mother never worked outside the home, and the family expectation was that her younger brother would go into the business. They didn't talk about money, but one day, "my dad was working on his balance sheet, and he made a mistake and threw it into the garbage. I fished it out and he caught me looking at it." This led to their first conversation about business, money, and finance. An unanticipated career path began to open for her.

In college, as she considered her career, it dawned on her that she liked the bank. She surprised her father and asked him if she could join when she graduated. He agreed and welcomed her with a message in the company newsletter, noting that she would work there for five years and then quit and start a family. Aghast, she confronted him. While she wanted a career there, and she didn't necessarily aim to become the CEO, though she didn't want to foreclose that possibility in advance.

Her brother worked there too, and he was expected to become the business leader. So, when they worked alongside each other, Arlene felt the sting of competition. She was asked to expand the business and felt capable, but she first worked it out with her brother. He went to work at another company the family owned, and they were able to remain close and talk every day, with each on their own turf. Arlene became the CEO a few years later, and now her son and daughter are in place to become the next generation of leaders.

Since the pioneering women's families didn't traditionally expect, or even allow women to enter the business, entry often originated from a special situation. It can happen through a family crisis, perhaps one that interferes with the expected succession process, which provides an opportunity that might not have happened otherwise.

One family, for instance, with a food-manufacturing business, had four young adult siblings, none working in the business. One of the siblings, Kathy, had asked her father several times about entering the business; he discouraged her. She and her husband later moved to the other coast, where their careers prospered. She found that she wanted to lead a company—and the family business was more attractive to her than the larger corporation where she worked. Finally, after the untimely death of her brother, the father relented and agreed for her to move back and enter the company. Cross-gender transitions are easier, because the edge of competitiveness is not there as much [as it would be with men]. Her father was uncomfortable with her entrepreneurial plans, and he ultimately agreed to sell her the business. Kathy didn't want to work with her siblings either, so she arranged to buy them out. This made everyone happy...and all were free to pursue their own directions.

Tradition also may be uprooted when a daughter is the only candidate. One young woman, Diane, from an old-money family had a family elder set her on her path. She recalled that when she was in business school her grandfather sought her out for dinner. He asked her to consider working with him in the family office. Other family members were all pursuing careers in community and environmental action or art, so he didn't see anyone in her generation who was interested in business. While she shared the family's social and environmental responsibility values, she felt called upon to take the role of business leader to serve the family. She clearly viewed her role as a servant leader, rather than as wanting power over the lives of her many cousins.

When there's no clear opportunity or lack of candidates, the daughter must prove herself in ways that a male heir might not have to. Entering the business is just a first step. To succeed, the daughter must next prove herself, perhaps as the first woman to perform such a role. One such example was the younger daughter of five siblings. Her father brought all his children to the business when they were growing up, but he didn't expect his daughter to enter it. She was a high achiever and very confident, and at first pursued a political career. The opportunity to manage the family office came suddenly. The other executives wondered "what the hell I was doing there," she said, having been raised "with the [traditional] expectation around me that I was to be a good wife and mother, but a recognition that I was smart and had ambitions. I was very much supported in these things—as long as they didn't threaten my role as a mother and wife." This expectation held true for most of the women we interviewed if they wanted to enter the new territory (for women) of family leadership.

> # For these daughters, entering the family business wasn't the starting point of a preordained path. Next came proving their worth in a historically patriarchal structure.

Another woman remembered that her father was not around for her and didn't consider women as candidates for work in the family enterprise. She knew she had talent and capability, but because "I didn't want to live my life having the main goal to prove to my father that I was worthy," she pursued her own career. Even so, she was rankled when her father invited her male cousin to enter the business and have an office next to his. She did eventually join the business and demanded that she get the same salary as her cousin. She did. They acted as equals, but she was more socially skilled, began to chair the meetings, and became more visible. She joined YPO (the Young Presidents Organization) and learned executive skills from their meetings. She's now seen as the leader but still works with her cousin collaboratively.

STAGE 3: BALANCING BUSINESS AND FAMILY RELATIONSHIPS

No matter what their leadership role, most of the women in our study actively raise their young children and allow their husbands to pursue their own careers. When a sister or daughter assumes leadership, their gender offers them both advantages and disadvantages. An older sister may become a natural family leader from childhood, or a younger sister may fall into a leadership role if her elders take other paths.

While it can also be true of male family successors, the women in our study had an especially deep concern for the harmony of the family, along with the entrepreneurial direction of their business leadership. One woman was able to harmonize the divergent talents and family expectations of her tough, financially oriented sister, her easy-going dependable but unimaginative brother, and her capable and sensitive husband. Her experience somewhat confirms the theory that there are fewer destructive sibling conflicts between a brother and sister than often emerge between two brothers.

Many women view their lives as posing an either-or choice: work in the family enterprise or focus on the family. If nothing else can be learned from our research, it's that this is a false dichotomy. Several of our women pioneers decided to leave the workforce when they had children, but this wasn't a permanent or irrevocable choice. Being natural leaders, they sometimes took on significant responsibility in the community and nonprofit worlds—which enabled them to develop skills and demonstrate leadership qualities. And they eventually took leadership roles in family governance, the business, or the family office. As one woman put it: "My life has had a lot of phases and I would say that you can have it all, just not all at the same time. I've had times in my life where I've been absolutely focused on family, times where I've been focused on community, and times when I've focused on my career. These three legs are not always in balance but over a lifetime they can be."

STORY 11:
Transforming Family Culture

If there are several siblings, a sister may emerge into leadership because she exhibits a special talent for diplomacy and an ability to balance efforts in several directions. A daughter in the family business doesn't run the business with the tunnel vision of an entrepreneur.

Mary has two sisters and a brother who grew up working together on the family's growing farm. "We grew up wealthy," she said, "but I was a farm kid and was expected to work." She learned to type and became her father's assistant. He grew up among strong women, and she saw that "gender roles applied at home, but we were more equal in the workplace." Like her siblings, Mary joined the business after college and never left. "I didn't choose the family business, it chose me," she noted. When she married, her husband also entered the business.

Mary's special skill was her ability to work with and tolerate her difficult father. He regularly dressed her down and never gave her credit for her achievements. But she was the only one in the family who could confront him, and she persisted. She succeeded because she didn't compete with him, just let issues go and did the right thing. She expanded the business, launched new products, and became president by the time she was forty.

Governing with a style opposite to her father, she listened to her siblings and her husband, creating an open and collaborative family culture. She doesn't dominate her siblings but sees them as stewards like her. Mary inaugurated family meetings and created advisory boards from the community and inside the company. She feels equal responsibility for the growth of the business and the harmony of the family. "By keeping the business together, you keep the family together and vice versa," she said. She is the family glue, embodying compromise and solving problems together.

Mary made several observations about the special role a daughter can take, highlighting the role of women as bridges to a more egalitarian family and business culture. "Women are more open and self-aware of their own abilities and have an openness to the needs of others, which lend themselves to taking on senior leadership roles within business families that will help to aid their success. They have these unique skills that are special to women and can combine those with other family members, including men. Households are more collaborative these days; both parents tend to work and both parents are expected to do their part and take care of the household, where before guys got a bit of a household free pass and the women who chose to work were expected to do both."

STAGE 4: MOVING INTO LEADERSHIP

When he's the original family enterprise leader, a father can be the CEO, president, and board chair—roles that aren't clearly differentiated—and he often expects, whether consciously or not, that his successor will also occupy all three. But, according to the women reporting on their relationship with the father, he might say: "Not right now." That's because the succession process can include a long transition of sharing power with their father, who, like many business founders, is reluctant to fully let go. Contradictorily, he expects the next-generation leader to defer to him and exercise firm leadership.

So, the traditional succession process isn't simply passing the baton from one generation to the next. There can be the long period of collaboration with the father; the good daughter can be willing to manage a difficult role as the family steward; or the female successor can simply emerge by doing a good job and becoming accepted as the new leader. Also, she might share leadership with a brother to avoid competition.

While first-generation leadership usually meant just running the family business, later generations often require outside business counsel and leadership. Leaders in these generations can then become the family office or board chair, a more flexible and less time-intensive position than a full-time CEO. These roles allow women leaders to combine parenting with the family enterprise and showcase their ability to bring family members together and work toward a common goal.

STORY 12:
From Mother to Daughter

All but one of our accounts refer to fathers as the original business leaders. In this exception, Lisa's mother was a second-generation daughter who took over the business from her father. Lisa in turn is in a second generation of daughters, and her mother arranged an orderly and collaborative succession process for her to become the leader.

Lisa's grandfather founded the business more than a century ago. After his two sons—her mother's brothers—decided they didn't want to run the business, their sister, a single mother of four young children, came back into town to run the business with her father. "Mom, through her love of going down to the business and being there and being at grandfather's side, gathered knowledge but also gathered the love of the company," Lisa recalled. "She always said, 'All the employees at the company were my fifth children.' She had this love for employees even though she was also tough and opinionated. She ended up buying the company from her brothers. She didn't intend to lead it but felt compelled to do it, even though she had only a high-school education." First, the company tried out several employees as CEOs, but then Lisa's mother just said, "I can do this."

Lisa added, "In the 1980s, that was quite a thing! You had this person chopping heads off executives who always had this deep love for the lowest of the low." Lisa had an older brother and sister and a younger sister, all of them raised on a farm next door to the factory. They lived frugally but their mother had a nanny to help her. "Mother instilled a love of the company in all her four children," Lisa said. "Her greatest gift to us is not about financials, it's about the employees. I think that's a side that maybe women see. I'm not saying men can't see it too. I have two boys and a daughter, and I tell them about this. When they were just out of school, she put all the siblings on the board."

As they grew up, only Lisa and her older sister maintained their interest in the business. Her sister was much like her mother, driven and opinionated. Lisa developed into the opposite, softer and more collaborative. And they had a non-family CEO who shared their commitment to a positive family culture. Lisa got some coaching from her own daughter to be more assertive, and after a struggle with her sister she has emerged as the family chair, succeeding her mother who is still active in her nineties! In the fourth generation, Lisa and her siblings have a family council and governance structure and expect to continue the business and keep a harmonious family as it enters a new generation of success. And Lisa, like her mother, is actively training and cultivating her daughters for future leadership.

In summary, rising generation women who ascend into formal family leadership in traditional family cultures define their leadership in four stages:

1. Making the choice to challenge the established culture

Growing up, young women usually don't expect to become family leaders, but they can develop self-confidence and drive to create a meaningful career. The traditional roles that are offered don't seem fulfilling, so they forge their own paths, and since they don't need to earn money, they do something that matters to them. By nature, they're driven and hardworking, but they need to find a direction for their energy. Some decide they want to become professionals and take on areas that were traditionally not open to a wealthy family's daughters. And they must discover and then demonstrate that they're serious and capable. Their work will likely begin outside the family orbit, but it'll further develop their confidence and capability, their will and skill.

2. Entering the family enterprise

At some point, the young woman sees the possibility of entering and ascending to leadership in the family enterprise. To be successful, some women actively initiate conversations about a leadership role, while others are chosen due to a crisis or because there's no one else available. They may learn informally and indirectly about the family enterprise, but it may not be clear whether there's a place for them or how to even ask about one. They may actively start the process by asking to learn more formally about the business (if there's one) or the family wealth. They can then expand their sense of what's needed and what's possible to legitimize their positive interest. Because their succession as a family leader (and not wanting a traditional role in the home) isn't expected, they have to ask for that role then have it accepted by their elders.

3. Balancing business and family relationships

The women we interviewed worked hard to balance their responsibilities in careers and business with an active role in the household. Inheriting ownership is not a passive process but includes the burden of taking an active leadership role as CEO or chairman in the family business, enterprise, or other career. In taking that role, these women are especially attuned to attaining a balance between leadership in the business, harmonious relationships with siblings and cousins, and raising the next generation. To make this happen, they see that the family needs to develop a capacity for communication, balance, and productive interaction. They're especially sensitive to these internal tensions and dynamics, reinforcing their commitment to relationship and feeling that they have to lead in these areas, or it will not happen.

4. Moving into leadership

If she's formally appointed the leader by the older-generation owners, the young woman takes the public steps of solidifying her leadership with actions such as buying the business from other family members, taking the wheel of the family office (or other structure), defining roles and authority with siblings, and finding ways to work in harmony with them. She leads actively in multiple areas of their lives, including raising children, bridging values, and building the family enterprise.

8

UNITING THE FAMILY THROUGH GOVERNANCE

Family governance has two key elements:

(1) defining practices for shared family activities and decision-making; and

(2) developing values and practices for education and advancement of the next generation.

Most of the families we studied established some form of governance in their second or third generations. And as champions of change in family culture, and in learning from past family conflict and unclear decision-making, the women inheritors played an active role in making that happen. An egalitarian culture in a family is defined by governance structures that affirm and recognize this reality, and the women leaders exercised leadership to redefine some of the ways that families make decisions about business and wealth.

Family governance differs from business and financial governance in that it refers to the organization, planning, and decision-making of purely family activities—which include family development, values, and policies for connection to their family enterprises. Such governance allows the family to transition into a different form by changing the structure and mix of its business and designing the family activities. The family members need to adapt to deal with the effects of any change in external conditions and then decide as a unit what they want for the future. Several of the families we studied either (1) sold their legacy family business, or (2) added a family office, charitable foundation, or other assets to the diversified family portfolio. These shifts were accompanied by an increase in family engagement and governance.

Family governance is unique from the principles established in the boardroom or bank. It refers to the organization, planning, and decision-making of purely family activities.

The women's role in governance creation often evolved organically—as a result of direct engagement with either a father who was a business leader or with her siblings. They experienced a need to convene as a family and ask questions about their future and how to achieve it. Third- or fourth-generation heirs are usually part of an extended family with several branches, and they need to address questions on whether the family desires to remain a shared entity and, if yes, in what form. The women we interviewed were acutely aware of the challenges facing their boys and girls, and they wanted to make sure that their children's path forward was clearer. They feared that the existing family model of informal decision-making and negotiation could lead to misunderstanding and competition. So, they wanted to make sure that there was a climate of fairness and opportunity for the most capable, whether male or female.

To accomplish these tasks, the women with larger families felt that their role as family culture leader included helping the family set up governance policies and practices to structure both their business and financial oversight, as well as non-business activities of their family. To develop a business board (sometimes with independent directors) and develop a family constitution, several of the families engaged a consultant. Such developments recognized values of collaboration, opened pathways to engagement for men and women, and acknowledged the mission and purpose of the family enterprise. They also defined clear and explicit policies and roles for participation in the family enterprise and in its benefits. By doing this work, the women hoped that the path forward for their daughters and sons would be less stressful and less ambiguous than their own. In this way, they institutionalized gender equality and family collaboration.

Family governance provides a setting in which the next-generation members can learn together as they take part in family activities and, potentially, in the family enterprise, while also pursuing their own careers. This rising generation needs to decide how separate they want each family member to become and what will be the nature and extent of their shared assets. As an example, one of the women's daughters living in a blended family with the husband's children created an engaged family culture of special meetings and openness—where there was none before. Issues such as shared assets could be discussed and resolved at these family meetings.

Developing family governance separately from the family's business and financial affairs is an added leadership responsibility. The women we interviewed naturally became governance champions, combining business with active family leadership. They're the leaders of preparing the rising generation in their roles as stewards and in leading their own careers. After they've established their leadership, this role is recognized as a definite family activity, not just a personal preference.

Such a role is essential to the family in transition; but it's not forever. Succession is also on these leaders' minds. They don't want to succeed a father who stayed on too long or just plug a vacuum in family leadership. After combining business and family leadership, one woman noted: "I would love to give up the family leader role to someone in the next generation. This role as Chief Emotional Officer looks out for the health and well-being of the family, to make sure that the family is cohesive, that we're pulling together, that we support each other, and that we're communicating with each other. It's not about the business. That's something my father never did, having family meetings and shared conversation."

This woman made an important observation about family meetings and joint decisions: that the family had to learn to recalibrate their relationships from parent/child to peers. "We spent most of the time introducing ourselves to each other as adults and not as my father's daughter or my aunt's niece or as the big sister," she said.

STORY 13:
Renewing a Shared Family Dream

This is the story of how one family developed and expanded its governance system, its business, and eventually its family enterprise.

Doris, a member of the family's third generation, succeeded her father as the CEO of the family enterprise, working with her three brothers. They began meeting informally every month, defining the group as a family council. As they began work with a consultant, they learned that this was just a first step. When a dozen members of their rising generation wanted to be included, they developed a more formal council with set terms and a board for the company that owns their family office. They now have an annual family-activity budget and, in the fall and spring, family town meetings—one with a business focus, the other for family activities.

When their operating business was sold, they realized that each family branch had different values and perspectives. Each branch was free to go its own way and, if they wished, each person could stay with the family group. One branch did choose to leave— they had different dreams. "Since the sale," Doris said, "the shared governance and activities haven't been about investment performance. They've been about what we care about as a family and how we're going to support those things whether it's philanthropy or a piece of undeveloped land."

Doris had four grown children when the family sold their operating business, but they maintained their own family office, shared with one of her brothers and his children. Impressively, after this significant liquidity event and in her 50s, she decided that to continue leading the family she would "return to school" to become a Certified Financial Planner™. Doris supported the children in pursuing their own aspirations—with the option of becoming involved in governance of the family enterprises. She noted that she wanted to "support them as they wandered from one thing to another and chose a path" and did so by making gifts of stock. She realized that many young people growing up with extensive family wealth have difficulty settling on a life path, and so she wanted to be sure to help them.

Under Doris's leadership, the family refashioned its governance structure to maintain relevance with the rising generation. It created a Unity Fund, a family fund with a pool of money to support shared activities. This offered the family members an incentive for deciding and working together on shared ventures, both financial and non-financial. The extensive family governance includes a family council, several committees, and an annual family assembly.

It has since made another shift to "interest-based governance," in which the family forms task forces to deal with set needs and asks the next generation to create strategic renewal for the future. Family members are invited to participate in these shared activities but aren't required. The activities include, for example, a group to deal with their foundation and another with the shared family yacht. Strategic renewal is being led and convened by the next generation, while Doris has stepped down as chair of the family council to make way for her oldest daughter, who's well prepared for the future.

THE FOUR LESSONS

Our interviews with daughters who become family leaders reveal a picture of a complex role spanning business and family. They don't see a strict boundary between the two, as they regard their leadership role as responsible for both. These pioneer women are sensitive to their pivotal role as a bridge between generations, ushering in new values, behavior, and expectations. Because the first-generation leaders didn't have a family enterprise history, their experience differs from these inheritors, though there are some common elements between the two situations. The stories of these next-generation family leaders offer four distinct lessons:

1. Navigating a journey of self-discovery and self-realization

These women had no well-worn path to follow; they had to invent their own. Early on, they sensed that they had talent and capability and found some encouragement from their fathers, the patriarchs. The paths they forged led them to develop their own careers, although circumstance and opportunity would lead them back to the family enterprise as they sought out and came into leadership of the business and the family.

2. Branding their own leadership style

They were often pioneering in their work and their business, taking on roles that were rarely occupied by women. They had to overcome resistance and skepticism, but they did so in their own style. Though some men have a similar style, all these women approached leadership with business values that were based on empathy and collaboration—within the family and with non-family employees. They were connectors even as they made hard choices and sometimes had to sell the business or take it in new directions.

3. Taking on a dual responsibility in family and work

While other couples may have a division of labor—the woman focused on family, the man on business—these women needed to lead in both areas. Their husbands had their own paths, but they, as the family heirs, felt a responsibility for raising their children as well as working. They championed values and developed governance practices to implement in the family.

4. Creating a family culture of openness and opportunities

They initiated talk of values and what it meant to be a member of the family, and they set up more opportunities to share those values in the family culture and its activities. Remembering their own challenges, they wanted to make sure their children adopted some of their values but were also free to go their own way, without gender limitations. They worked hard to create a family culture of openness, respect for everyone's talents, and free choice on what to do.

Their families weren't usually set up for collaboration or participation. The women were often born into patriarchal families that didn't expect to share information, and in which the elders expected the ability to select successors using traditional criteria. Facing these obstacles, they had to turn inward, toward themselves, and find the confidence and drive to challenge and prevail. They found help and support from others, both from within the family and from their advisors. But they had to take initiative themselves to forge their own paths. If they had a lack of confidence, they had to overcome it alone.

We admire the readiness of these women to overcome obstacles that stood in their way with a calm determination and steadiness. Each woman faced some resistance in becoming a leader of the family, the business, or both. They faced resistance from parents who held traditional views of what a woman should do, from male siblings who felt their sisters shouldn't be engaged in business, and from employees and the community—neither of which were comfortable with women as leaders.

Given the adversity they faced, these women felt a responsibility to make sure that the next generation faced a family more open to and more accepting of gender equality. They know they're in the middle of a generational and societal transformation, and they use their personal journeys to advance the fairness and equality between men and women, and develop a family culture of transparency, collaboration, and stewardship.

PART III

applying
the lessons

9

BRIDGE TO THE FUTURE

Even as they were active in their own careers or managing the family enterprise, the women we interviewed in all generations felt a special responsibility to help their rising generations prepare for the future in a new way. Both the women of the wealth-creating generation and later generations had a deep desire to pass their values and wisdom to their daughters (and sons). They didn't want a repeat of their own difficult experiences, in which their preparation and education either didn't exist at all or were painful, demoralizing, even scary and lonely. Most of them were highly motivated by what was not done for them when they were growing up: they hadn't felt supported in learning how to take care of the wealth, let alone manage money in the context of supporting traditional family responsibilities. Having overcome obstacles and resistance, they wanted their daughters to have a fairer, more-balanced playing field. They were especially aware of the need to teach their daughters that they had equal status and could actively prepare their offspring for productive lives and possible engagement in the family enterprise.

The split focus between work and the home is considered natural for women and isn't something they want to escape. It's probably reasonable to say that this was less of a concern for family patriarchs. Of the women we interviewed, most combined their family-enterprise work with raising kids, although some left the family enterprise (business, family office, or financial management) for a period of time to focus on their children. But given their drive and know-how, they also tended to move into community leadership. When their children became older, some of the women returned to work with the family, though often in a governance rather than an operational role. Those from old-money families may not have had family businesses to enter, but they still found roles in the community or with philanthropic work while raising their children or stepchildren.

These women were all change leaders, determined to use their experience as wealth-creators or inheritors in a shifting family culture, and to apply their knowledge of family across many generations to pave a new way for their kids. The concern was equally expressed by first-generation women and inheritors from later generations; their leadership led them to pay special attention to the mentoring and development of their rising generations. They wanted their achievement to be integrated into the family culture. The first-generation matriarchs felt that the preparation and focus on their children was the essence of their leadership; if they were business leaders, they acted in this role as stewards for their children.

Women from later generations tapped into their own dealings with inherited wealth and their self-awareness of what that wealth meant to them and how they found their voice and their role. They were able to provide more clarity on what change needed to look like to help their next-generation children flourish despite their great wealth and limit the impact of the traditional obstacles they had experienced. In other words, they didn't want the difficult journeys they had charted to be for naught.

> **Women from later generations were cognizant of their paths to a powerful, purposeful role in the family. They found clarity in how best to lay a similar path for the next generation.**

Having experienced the impacts of wealth, all these women developed the wisdom to "see around the corner." They experienced both the pain and the blessings of wealth and used that knowledge to prepare their children and grandchildren in an intentional way. As they set out to ensure that the next generation understands what's coming down the line, good and bad, these women have used their experience as wealth owners or heirs to teach their children seven lessons:

1. Encourage self-discovery

With a tone of what could be interpreted as cautionary, based on their own experiences, most of the women we interviewed advocate that the next generation be given the opportunity to create their own identity. These inheritors are aware that members of the rising generation need to decide independently what role they want to pursue. They understand that there are two important incentives for their children: they not only want to find their own individual path in life but also maintain their connection with the multi-generational family legacy—and maybe have a role in it.

One woman talked openly about the difficulty in doing this, because it was said publicly that she was the "heir to the great X fortune, and thus she has no cares." Her challenge was to find her own unique identity despite wanting to be given a choice between her personal path and engagement with her family. Other women, who want their children to have a life in which they're separate but connected, realize that this will take a lot of work on their part. They need to teach their children to collaborate and work together, even as they're doing other things and finding their own path.

The major concern of parents with substantial wealth is that their children become entitled about having free access to their wealth. They want their children to be frugal and responsible, and consider themselves stewards of the family wealth, with a responsibility to pass it on to their children, even as they enjoy its benefits in their own lives. The most successful begin teaching and modeling those values early and make these lessons an integral part of their parenting.

2. Refresh and model values

When asked the most important thing they can do for their children, most of the mothers replied: provide clarity and teach and model commitment about values and what matters most. Those who came from multi-generational families of wealth typically held strong values, rooted in tradition. In some cases, traditional values such as secrecy and avoiding discussion of wealth had a high cost. They re-thought those values for the new social situation and were willing and courageous enough to challenge them. They took seriously their roles as models for and teachers of those values to ensure that the next generation is clear about expectations for leadership. In either case, they were more open to hearing how the next generation interprets those values; and when those views didn't make sense to them, they were willing to challenge different interpretations of shared values and work hard to reach shared understanding.

Our matriarchs and successors wanted to ensure that their families understood their values and hoped that the next-generation inheritors use them as their compass too. Those most effective at this were the women who used their practices as a means of modeling and teaching their children common values about wealth: transparency, getting involved in family governance and activity, being a contributor not just a beneficiary, making a difference, and living a frugal and thoughtful life.

3. Teach a stewardship mindset

In their role as family culture change leaders, several women talked about what it means to be a steward rather than an owner of wealth. Unless active wealth-creation took place across generations, these women were concerned about the responsibility of ensuring that wealth exists in future generations. Given the challenge of being a great distance from the wealth and its creation, they worked to define and then set the expectations of stewardship: being informed and taking part in a shared family mission and family activities; and taking a broad view of wealth and its place in their lives. They've been active in transforming an owner mindset into a stewardship mindset while at the same time supporting wealth-creation goals their children may have for themselves. This process was more than just good intentions; they dedicated a great deal of energy, time, and focus to making it happen.

One third-generation daughter learned the value and responsibility of finances, along with independence from her very successful father, while being raised in a traditional family household in which men were the providers. After she met her husband when her career was taking off, she agreed, with a tinge of regret, to step off the career track and take on the traditional role of motherhood. She made sure that her daughters grew up with a strong sense of independence, a sound personal financial responsibility, and a sense of what it means to be a steward. She also encouraged them with what was less available to her generation: gender equality in marriage.

All three daughters are now extremely well-educated and working mothers. They were raised to not only be stewards of the family wealth but also be committed to their own wealth creation—in a new generation that makes working motherhood more accessible, and more accepted. While family resources made many options possible, her daughters were raised to follow their own passions (in community service, business, finance, or philanthropy) and were expected to do something active and useful in addition to any family responsibility around wealth stewardship.

4. Reignite an entrepreneurial spirit

While re-creating wealth to sustain the family for generations to come was on the minds of our matriarchs, ideas around entrepreneurship and other wealth-creation activities were often used, as one woman suggested, as a "great teacher." She was committed to educating and engaging her children through entrepreneurism. Another woman, who passed on her position as the CEO of her family manufacturing business to a non-family CEO and became board chair of their family office, wants to expand into investments in other companies. As a result, she feels like a first-generation wealth creator rather than second generation and wants to pass on that entrepreneurial spirit to her son and daughter. She has had many talks with them on the role of money and possible directions for the family to take and has created an education program for them and their cousins. Her goal is to inspire them to find roles in family investment and the family office, but she's patient as they pursue pathways for their own careers. She wants them to see the family business as an option, not an expectation. Another of the women with school-age children takes them on family trips, is teaching them to be good shareholders, and is developing a special place for the family to be together.

5. Open to a new meaning for "staying together"

Our inheritors understood from their own experiences that if they choose not to work together, the shared elements of the family can drift apart and not continue. To that end, several women mentioned that they needed to be open to a new meaning for "staying together", and not remain stuck on what has been the historical perspective of how they stay together. They embrace new skills of compromise with their children and explore and consider new ways of working together.

After being instrumental in overcoming significant conflict with her father and in working with her siblings, one family CEO noted, "My role was given to me by my family; but I know that by keeping the business together, you keep the family together, and vice versa. My siblings and I are partners in the business [that] we were given together." This woman, who has worked hard to create a positive culture in the next generation, is the glue for the family in the new generation, notably teaching and modeling the ability to compromise—"the ability and willingness to compromise and find a solution that is going to be amenable to everyone."

6. Serve as mentors

These first generation and successor leaders were viewed as role models and examples by their children, especially their daughters. If they came from a traditional family, their example made it clear that daughters were not subordinate and could avail themselves of the same choices as their male siblings. As the children became adults, their mothers acted not only as role models but also in more proactive roles as mentors. They take the lessons they learned from their parents (and from their own experiences) to work with their daughters, and with their sons, to set new expectations and values in the family culture. They see family leadership as not just taking care of the various enterprises but also taking time to develop their rising generation. They really understand the importance of culture and become more intentional about teaching "the how" to their offspring.

7. Right past "wrongs"

For some of the older women in our study, attention to stewarding future generations extended quite dramatically to their grandchildren. They spoke openly about their mistakes and what they wish they could have done better. One grandmother in a blended family with a large inheritance said, "Part of my passion for being a grandmother is that I was not a passionate mother in ways I should have been and it's almost like I have an opportunity to do it again." Another woman with a similar family noted that as a matriarch and grandmother, her children, grandchildren, and in-laws all regard her as a person they can trust, one they can consult. As a non-parent relative, she can listen to difficult issues and help them from a less emotionally exposed place. And listening to all these women, it was particularly poignant to hear of their vulnerability and honesty—over the years and over the generations—and how, now, they seek to find peace in some of their decisions and to work hard to be a voice that helps their progeny bridge better to the future.

Women family leaders don't just lead and develop the family enterprise, they feel called upon to extend the new values of the collaborative family culture to their children and grandchildren. They take the time and develop the activities to teach and continue the innovation that they pioneered.

> # Some of the older women exuded vulnerability with each word, reflecting on mishaps and mistakes as the learnings so rich and valuable in building trusted relationships with their grandchildren.

10

PERSONAL IMPACT OF ADVISORS

The role of advisors engendered mixed reactions from the women leaders we interviewed. Some count on their advisors as notable partners, key players, or advocates. Other women, however, find that their legacy advisors—those they inherited or other long-standing advisors—don't make the shift they need. That's probably because those advisors continue to conduct and manage the relationship just as they did under prior leaders, often the patriarchs or patriarchal figures. We concluded that the most successful advisors to these female family leaders are those that do two very important things:

(1) take the time to help them understand all aspects of the family enterprise, including its wealth structures and their financial implications; and

(2) empower these women to make their own decisions.

The women in our study rarely seek advisors who make all the decisions for them; and they desire reasonable understanding. They feel that the stakes are higher for them in advisor selection and management as opposed to the scenario for men in their families, especially when they're experiencing change, sensing conflict, or anticipating unknown territory. It's often daunting or intimidating for them to decide "what to do with the family wealth" and also receive financial and family support, especially if the management of the wealth falls on their shoulders. These women believe the stakes are higher for them because they've found few, if any, great female role models. So here, too, they've had to be pioneers.

On top of this, the pressure can be oppressive due to "issues" with their children or grandchildren, their health, or their aptitude, given the traditional role these women have played in their families. In leadership roles in their family enterprise, they seek advisors who can manage the wealth and care for the family by addressing their needs for education around wealth and teaching them how to make decisions about wealth for the family. Fear and resentment of advisors' judgment, or frustration with their talking "only numbers" and not taking the time and interest to understand their "bigger issues," have become non-starters for many female leaders.

LESSONS FOR ADVISORS

When asked what they want from an advisor, the women we interviewed mentioned the following observations and preferences:

1. Shed legacy-advisory mindset

One woman, who emerged as the family leader when her husband passed away, removed the white-shoe team after several months of working with them. While it was a technically strong team of advisors, she found they continued in a traditional "caretaking" role and didn't want to make changes in managing her relationship. "I didn't want to be only taken care of," she said. "I wanted to learn and become more confident with decisions."

2. Capitalize on coaching

It's been noted that women tend to be more open to the concept of coaching—most likely due to how they've been socialized over generations. Those women who found that their advisors served more as coaches than "advisors" had greater success in achieving their goals of understanding the wealth and feeling good about the decisions related to the wealth and family. One older woman greatly appreciated an advisor who was younger in his career but more open to working alongside women (likely due to his generational experience), because he helped her learn and grow into her role and responsibilities. He served as supporter and teacher, walking alongside her as she worked to understand what she needed to do to shepherd her family. He shared her view of power and influence, working alongside not over others.

3. See and share *their* future

The women of wealth agreed that the best advisor is the one who can help them see their future in a big-picture way, inclusive of *all* their roles as a leader, mother, grandmother, career woman, and so on. One woman called this type of advisor as "life-changing." But given their experience, such an advisor relationship was not accessible to all of them. "I never expected to find an advisor who introduced the consequences and implications of an extremely complex set of circumstances, opening my eyes to my personal unknowns—[someone who could also] hold my hand or lead me along with the confidence that I really needed given the terrible pressure I felt," another woman said. "I was confident and successful in my career, but I didn't have that same confidence when it came to my wealth."

4. "Lean in" to both spouses

While a husband was generally open to and welcomed the partnership of his wife, their most highly valued advisors were the ones who proactively worked in terms of shared understanding and decision-making for both spouses. "My advisor appreciated that my husband wanted me to learn, even though it slowed us down and the advisor had to explain more, do more, work harder," one woman said. "They weren't reluctant, and were even willing to lean-in, to bring us together and get us aligned. ...I found this especially interesting when they had to navigate conversations that were more important to me than they were to my husband. My husband was open to welcoming them, and my advisor picked right up on that." Others noted their surprise and delight when that rare advisor didn't wait for the invitation, but gently urged the wife's participation.

5. Represent like-minded female leadership

Two families changed advisors because they wanted to find someone who would work well with family members from all generations. One woman shared that she and her husband first "tested" advisors and their commitment to the female members of her family. Would they receive similar support and development over time? In the end, they liked best the female leaders in the advisory firm—both for their influence and their commitment to educate the children. Many couples now have, as a discrete criterion for engagement, a requirement to have female advisors and an assurance that their female children will have a voice.

6. Honor the family and its dynamics

In ways that were often not as important to their spouses, our women participants sought out advisors who both understood the family dynamics and served as financial leaders. One multigenerational family, bound by a large family trust, experienced significant sibling conflict in which some voices rang louder than others. For those who felt disenfranchised, enormous comfort and reassurance was created by advisors who worked in both a "family" and an "individual household" capacity, cognizant of the differences. The advisor impact was unquestionably more successful for those advisors who became extremely adept at navigating both wealth and family concerns.

Demonstrating actual success in working with these female leaders, not just paying lip service, underpins the collective voice of the women in our study. And there's a central message sent to the advisor community: grow with the times and provide highly customized and thoughtful service to women family leaders. They're finding their voice and want to be heard.

11

CONCLUSION: INSIGHTS ON THE "NEW MATRIARCHS"

After speaking to so many women leaders, a fuller, deeper, and richer picture of family enterprise has emerged. We see family enterprise as more than a wealth-producing business or family office with a family loosely attached. Instead, by adding the perspective of women leaders, we can see how much its destiny and success is tied to that of the family. Accounts of family enterprise have tended to over-emphasize the male and business elements. Our research offers more balance, as we add the influential role of women and initiating family engagement and development to the mix.

When we view the family enterprise through the eyes of women leaders, their story looks very different than what's seen through the eyes of male business leaders. We cannot understand women's reality without the lens of gender roles and differences. While gender is not destiny, and today, the roles and opportunities of men and women are becoming more equal, the reality is that men and women are different and tend to have different mindsets, concerns and operate differently from each other. By taking the focus off male leadership and looking at the many ways that women in older and younger generations exercise leadership, we see a different, maybe broader, picture of what leadership can be.

Our research suggests that there are some clear differences in what men and women need to learn to become better leaders in the family enterprise; men need to learn to listen and express openness to others' ideas, while women need to learn to value their selves and their contributions. These are common gender themes, but the crucible of the family enterprise creates opportunities for each gender to learn and overcome their weak spots.

There's a global movement underway to narrow the vast difference in power and opportunity for women. A century ago, rigidly defined gender roles, legally defined, were the norm. Over time, the differences and barriers to leadership roles and equal inheritance have diminished. But our research takes place in a social environment where gender roles are under debate and in flux. Our research has caught this evolution at a moment in time, and within families where these traditions and debates are ongoing. These "new matriarchs" are bending the arc of traditional gender roles—not by completely shunning the traditional matriarchal construct, but by claiming their ability to reshape it as both caretakers and corporate leaders, family stewards and financial stakeholders. They're advocates and models of greater equality, as well as examples of what women's sensitivity and gender experience can bring to family leadership. Within the family enterprise, we can see close up the dynamics of this societal evolution, and how women are often the initiators of innovation and change in their families.

Each section focused on one generational experience. Across them, five interconnected themes about the nature of women leaders in family enterprise emerged:

WOMEN AS BRIDGE BUILDERS AND CONNECTORS

Women are "bridge builders", connecting individuals between business and family, and across generations. Their attention as leaders is less focused on their internal vision and more on everyone else—family members older and younger, employees, customers, and community. They see alignment and connection as the key to success. Their vision comes from their deep sense that the family enterprise is something that's to be shared and used wisely. Being a leader, to them, isn't just a business role—it's about harmony and connection between business and family. If one isn't thriving, the other loses its value.

There are two common views of leadership, and while they aren't necessarily gender-based, much evidence and experience suggest that they can be tied to gender-based styles. The heroic view of leadership is the leader as a lone warrior, forging ahead with such power and authority that he inspires everyone to follow. They're different from others, separate, and follow their inner authority; their followers are privileged to have such a leader as he helps them reach success that they couldn't ever have achieved on their own. Business mythology tends to embrace the heroic story; and accounts by business founders about their achievements tend to reinforce this mythos. They tend to internalize this view in their own self-image, making them dominate and follow their own inner voice.

There's another, almost opposite, model that underpins the role that the women in our study pursued. These women exemplify an alternate view of leadership: stewardship, servant leadership, and leading from behind. In this view, the leader isn't separate, autonomous, and self-directed. Rather, leadership stems from their ability to sense what others need, inspire them, and exude a sense of connection, and shared purpose. They're moved by others and listen to them and act on their concerns. They may have a vision for the business but they're always aware of how their actions impact their family and those around them, and are able to listen and act on this sensitivity. This connected leadership was how the model was described by our women leaders in all generations.

CREATORS OF AN INCLUSIVE AND FAIR FAMILY CULTURE

Women don't differentiate sharply between family and business; their leadership tends to enhance both realms and bring them together. They aren't just concerned with their own leadership, but that they open the paths for other family members to participate. They feel that the purpose of the business and the family's wealth is to include and support everyone in the family, and to do so fairly. They tend to notice when others are in distress and seek to build fairness and inclusion everywhere.

Their leadership, as a co-founder, widow, or a next-generation leader, often includes peacemaking and helping overcome or heal family rifts and hurts that pulled otherwise successful families apart. They're selected for leadership by their family because of their ability to heal and collaborate. While many families are hurt by competition across generations or between siblings, the women leaders we interviewed tended to work hard to overcome these rivalries.

LEADERS USING SOFT POWER AND INFLUENCE RATHER THAN DOMINATION

Women have less need for the limelight and visible leadership; they tend to lead more quietly and behind the scenes. They influence others rather than try to overpower or force them into acquiescence; they're coalition builders across branches, generations and from family to business.

This sometimes leads to their contributions not being seen and appreciated. Women can ascend to leadership because they're able to make connections, work with difficult situations, and reach out to include others. They're mediators between family members, branches, generations, business, and family. They're often selected for leadership because of their quiet, inclusive style, that allows more family members to feel comfortable participating in family governance.

WOMEN HAVE THE INNER CONFIDENCE TO OVERCOME OBSTACLES WITHOUT ACRIMONY

While more families are accepting and inviting women into leadership positions, their path to leadership includes more pitfalls, challenges, and hurdles than their male counterparts. They sometimes struggle being seen as candidates for leadership. They don't tend to become bitter or resentful but accept that the family is evolving in its acceptance of women in key leadership roles. They were aware that the march to gender equality was taking place and that they were taking a step forward that must transfer to their children.

They've grown up with a sense of self-confidence and a feeling of personal efficacy and drive early in life. They had a feeling of acceptance in the family, or in their marriage to an entrepreneurial husband, that gave them the motivation and persistence to face and overcome barriers to leadership that may not affect their male peers, siblings, or cousins. This confidence allowed them to feel comfortable as innovators and pioneers in the family, and make sure that their success is also open to their daughters and sons. They want to see their achievements sustained by the behavior and expectations of their children and grandchildren.

USING WHAT WE LEARNED

The women in our study all hold an integrated, connected, inclusive, and meaningful view of the rationale and possibilities of family enterprise. By listening to them, we see how families can use their wealth in a way that creates harmony rather than division. Their sensitivity and struggle offer a picture of leadership that connects family and business. By hearing their stories, we learn about families that have been able to grow and innovate, at a time when resiliency and adaptation is necessary for every family enterprise. We hope that every family enterprise can learn from these stories, and even measure themselves against some of the yardsticks that the families in these pages have proposed.

ABOUT THE AUTHORS

Amy Hart Clyne

Amy Hart Clyne has dedicated her career to helping prosperous families fulfill the promise and potential of their legacies. As Chief Knowledge and Learning Officer at Pitcairn, Amy empowers wealthy families through family education while pioneering research and best practices that elevate the role of advisors to one of true partnership.

Before joining Pitcairn, Amy served as Executive Director and Chief Knowledge Officer at Family Office Exchange (FOX), where she led the organization's knowledge, learning, and education strategies for over 400 families and 150 multi-disciplinary advisors. Today, she leads Pitcairn's Gen7 Project®, the firm's thought leadership and learning lab providing unique resources, actionable content, and educational tools to families undergoing major wealth transitions. As an expert in private wealth management, Amy has spent her career translating the needs and desires of ultra-wealth families and their advisors into practical insights and solutions-based experiences that educate, excite, and engage.

Amy has an MBA in Marketing from Columbia Business School, Columbia University, and a bachelor's degree in international relations from Colgate University. She holds the designation of CERTIFIED FINANCIAL PLANNER™ and is a Certified Family Business Advisor.

Dennis T. Jaffe

Dennis T. Jaffe, Ph.D., Senior Research Fellow at Banyan Global Family Enterprise Consulting, is a San Francisco-based advisor to families about family business, governance, wealth, and philanthropy. He is author of *Borrowed from Your Grandchildren: The Evolution of 100-Year Family Enterprises (Wily, 2000); Cross Cultures: How Global Families Negotiate Change Across Generations (2016); Stewardship in your Family Enterprise: Developing Responsible Family Leadership Across Generations (Stewardship in Your Family Enterprise, 2014), and Working With the Ones You Love (2014).*

Dennis is a research associate at Wise Counsel Research, where he leads their 100-Year Family Enterprise Research Program. He is also Family Business Fellow at the Smith Family Business Program at Cornell University, a faculty advisor at the *Ultra High Net Worth Institute*, a regular contributor to *Forbes Leadership channel*, reporting on family cross-generational family business and wealth, and a professional member of *STEP, Society for Trust and Estate Planners*.

He was honored in 2020 with the award as individual thought leader in the field of wealth management by the *Family Wealth Report* and named as one of a hundred global influencers of family enterprise by the UK newsletter *Family Capital*. The Family Firm Institute awarded him the 2017 International Award for service, and in 2005 he received the Beckhard Award for service to the field. He has a BA degree in Philosophy, MA in Management, and Ph.D. in sociology, all from Yale University, and is professor emeritus of organizational systems and psychology at Saybrook University in San Francisco.

REFERENCES

1 https://www.barrons.com/articles/the-world-now-has-100-self-made-female-billionaires-01584390323

2 https://nces.ed.gov/fastfacts/display.asp?id=98

3 Barclays Private Bank, "Smarter Succession: The Challenges and Opportunities of Intergenerational Wealth Transfer," November 2020. https://privatebank.barclays.com/news-and-insights/2020/november/smarter-succession/challenges-and-opportunities/

4 The power of women in family business (November 2020), STEP-KPMG. (https://assets.kpmg/content/dam/kpmg/xx/pdf/2020/12/the-power-of-women-in-family-business.pdf)

5 Rosplock, Kirby, The Complete Family Office Handbook, 2nd Ed.: Wiley, 2021.

6 Rosplock, Kirby, Gender Matters: Men's and Women's Perceptions of Wealth are Mostly Aligned. *Journal of Wealth Management*, Spring, 2010.

7 James Grubman's *Strangers in Paradise* depicts the cultural and personal differences in the life and family experience of the first and later generations of wealthy families. This publication further explores the female roles in these generations.

8 Katy Danco (1981), *From the Other Side of the Bed: A Woman Looks at Life in the Family Business*. Cleveland, OH: The University Press.

9 Ernesto J Poza and Tracey Messer (2001) "Spousal Leadership and Continuity in the Family Firm." *Family Business Review*, Vol. 14, No. 1.

10 Jian Bai Li and Henning Piezunka, (2020). "The Uniplex Third: Enabling Single-domain Role Transitions in Multiplex Relationships," *Administrative Science Quarterly*. 85:2. Pp. 314-358.

11 Dennis Jaffe (1991). *Working with the Ones You Love*. Conari Books, Berkeley, CA. Chapter 5 talks about the nature of this role that spans both family and business.

12 This point has been made in other research, including the work in the seminal book, "Women's Ways of Knowing: The Development of Self, Voice, and Mind," by Mary Field Belenky and associates, first published by Basic Books in 1986.

13 Barnes, Louis B., Incongruent Hierarchies: Daughters and Younger Sons as Company CEOs: Family Business Review, 1:1, March, 1988.